Educating the Scholar Practitioner in Organization Development

A volume in
Contemporary Trends in Organization Development and Change

Series Editors
Peter Sorensen and Therese Yaeger, *Benedictine University*

Contemporary Trends in
Organization Development and Change

Peter Sorensen and Therese Yaeger, Series Editors

Educating the Scholar Practitioner in Organization Development

by

Deborah A. Colwill
Asbury Theological Seminary

Information Age Publishing, Inc.
Charlotte, North Carolina • www.infoagepub.com

Library of Congress Cataloging-in-Publication Data

Colwill, Deborah A.
Educating the scholar practitioner in organization development / by
Deborah A. Colwill.
p. cm. -- (Contemporary trends in organization development and
change)
Includes bibliographical references.
ISBN 978-1-61735-665-0 (pbk.) -- ISBN 978-1-61735-666-7 (hbk.) -- ISBN
978-1-61735-667-4 (ebook)
1. Organizational change--Study and teaching (Higher) 2. Organizational
behavior--Study and teaching (Higher) I. Title.
HD58.8.C644 2011
658.4'060711--dc23

2011039439

Printed in the United States of America

CONTENTS

CHAPTER 1

INTRODUCTION

The field of organizational development (OD) is a relatively young social science.[1] As such, OD continues to define its place in the broader worlds of the academy and practice (Burke, 2006). Over the past few decades, one evidence that the field is maturing is the emergence of doctoral programs specializing in organization development. These doctoral programs are training the scholars and practitioners who will likely provide much of the future leadership of this field on the near horizon. Presuming that doctoral students in OD will be leaders of future learning, the investment in their development is crucial. In addition since OD is a comparatively young social science, the intentional development of OD practitioners in a broader context outside higher education is also a necessary endeavor to advance the field. A closer look at these doctoral programs is warranted in order to gain a clear understanding of the potential influence they may have on the field of OD through their graduates. Likewise gleaning insight from the education of OD doctoral students may prove to be helpful in training OD practitioners outside of higher education.

The focus of this work explores the education of scholar practitioners in organization development. As alluded to above, one avenue of developing scholar practitioners in OD has been the professional research doctoral degree.[2] The research upon which this document is based examined the impact that professional research doctoral programs had on the learning and professional development of select doctoral graduates (Colwill, 2011). The twofold purpose of this research was to look at the intended learning outcomes of professional research doctoral programs[3] as reported by faculty, and to explore the perceptions of doctoral alumni regarding their

Educating the Scholar Practitioner in Organization Development, pp. 1–7

educational experience and how it contributed to their development as well as their current professional role. The research project was qualitative in nature and utilized in depth interviews as the main source of data. Four professional research doctoral programs affiliated with the field of OD participated in the study. From these four schools a total of 54 people were interviewed (18 faculty members and 36 alumni). A more detailed description of the research design and methodology is included in Appendix 1.

TWO GAPS IN THE CURRENT LITERATURE

In addition to the twofold purpose stated above, one of the rationales for this study was to investigate two specific gaps in the current literature. The first literature gap was found in the field of organization development. Whereas lists of OD competencies have been researched and articulated (Cummings & Worley, 2009), very little has been written on the intentional development of the OD professional. This work begins to address the first literature gap by exploring the significant learning of doctoral graduates during their educational experience which sheds light on some of the impactful ways these individuals have been developed. A second gap exists in the broader educational literature. More specifically, while there is ample research investigating undergraduate student development, very little research explores the development of doctoral students (Gardner & Mendoza, 2010). Both of these literature gaps are explored in more detail below.

Research on the Development of OD Professionals

The literature on OD practitioners is primarily characterized by "broadly framed competency clusters" and "general advice about achieving success in the field" (Kahnweiler, 2006, p. 11). For example, Cummings and Worley (2009) summarize four overarching categories that encompass most of what is written on OD practitioner competencies: (a) "intrapersonal skills," (b) "interpersonal skills," (c) "consulting skills," and (d) "knowledge of organization development theory" (p. 53). These categories provide a broad framework for understanding what OD professionals need to effectively practice their discipline. Another example comes from Worley and Feyerherm (2003) who interviewed 21 of the founders of the field of OD. The founders were asked, "What are the key skills, knowledge, values, or competencies that have made you successful?" (p. 103). The themes that emerged were "broad education, training, and experience", "interpersonal skills," "clear knowledge of self," "ability to see systems," "focusing on relevant issues," "ability to operate within values," "specific competences," "luck and timing," "exposure to the field," "cultural experience," and "theory and practice" (p. 103). The study by Worley and Feyerherm is helpful in gathering together the wisdom of some of the founding OD professionals. In addition, the study provides a starting place to articulate potential learning outcome themes for OD professionals. However, what contributed to the success of these seasoned veterans in the field may or may not continue to be applicable for the next generation of OD professionals. Many of the themes may be timeless, yet one wonders what may be missing from the perspective of looking backward in time as to what could be essential for the next season of practice and scholarship. As Conger and Xin (2000) state "we must not only train for current competencies but also anticipate and train for future competencies" (p. 98). In addition, listing and describing essential competencies does not equate with the know-how or ability to develop them. To the point, very little literature exists on the development of the OD professional (Kahnweiler, 2006; Worley & Feyerherm, 2003). This work hopes to shed some light on this issue. A second gap in the literature exists regarding the development of doctoral students. The following section explores the gap more fully.

Research on Doctoral Graduates

Upon graduation, the traditional career path for a doctoral student was to enter the academy as a junior faculty member; however in actuality, many doctoral graduates do not pursue careers in higher education (Golde & Walker, 2006). Recent research "indicated that fewer than half of the U.S. doctoral graduates surveyed take up career positions as academics" (Lee & Boud, 2009, p. 19). With such a large percentage of doctoral graduates not pursuing academic occupations, it is startling that two of the major criticisms against U.S. doctoral students are that they are believed to be: (a) educated too narrowly, and (b) lack necessary professional skills for the workplace such as the capacity to collaborate effectively, the ability to work in teams, and the capability to manage others (Nerad, 2008; Nerad & Heggelund, 2008). Whether or not these graduates intend on having a career in the academy or not, if these criticisms are true the resultant behavior of these graduates will greatly affect their abilities to build professional relationships with their colleagues and work effectively in their chosen fields. Golde (2006) agrees that many doctoral recipients "are ill-prepared to function effectively in the settings in which they work" (p. 5). One author states that the overarching problem with doctoral education is that it tends to be "divorced from postdoctoral reality" (C. Taylor, 2009, p. 48). Constructing doctoral programs that more effectively attend to preparing students for several types of career paths seems to be in order. The changing demands and pressures on doctoral education to service different career needs of students has put the traditional model of doctoral education in question (Gilbert, 2004). The effectiveness of doctoral programs "in the context of career success" is still uncertain today (Williamson, 2009, p. xviii).

In a general sense, research on doctoral education has increasingly grown over the past decade (Lee & Boud, 2009; Nerad, 2008). Despite the increase in research, the developmental needs of the doctoral student, have not yet been thoroughly examined (Gardner, 2009b). Anecdotally speaking, Damrosch (2009) states that graduate programs are "generally not very good at keeping in touch with alumni" (p. 36). As a consequence, "what is particularly lacking is any serious effort to engage many of those former students in the conversation about how to improve doctoral education" (C. Taylor, 2009, p. 54). The views of alumni are essential to improve the practice of doctoral education. Yet, very little is written about doctoral alumni's perceptions of their educational experience and how it contributes to their development and their current professional role. To date, no example of this type of study could be found within the field of organization development. However other examples do exist in the broader literature outside of OD, yet the findings of many of these studies are particular to the industry, field, or personal characteristics of the participants and thus not directly transferable to the world of OD.[4]

The above criticism of U.S. doctoral students' capabilities, the changing landscape of postdegree career choices of alumni, and the lack of information gleaned from alumni regarding their educational experiences highlight the need to take a closer look at the perspectives of successful[5] doctoral graduates. More specifically, feedback from these doctoral alumni regarding their educational experience would be beneficial in rethinking learning outcomes for doctoral education. Given the importance of developing doctoral students as the current and future scholars and practitioners of the field, the need for this type of study that investigates the education of scholar practitioner in OD is clear.

POTENTIAL CONTRIBUTION OF THE RESEARCH

Keeping in mind the two literature gaps described above, this research project has several points of potential significance. First, interviews with faculty highlighted both the deeply held values of the field of organization development, as well as the current educational strategies and practices used in professional research doctoral programs. The faculty perspectives underscored how and toward what the doctoral students are being intentionally shaped as professionals as well as how they are socialized into the field. A second point of potential significance from the study is that the alumni report important elements of their educational experience that contributed to their professional and personal growth. Both the intended and *hidden curriculum*[6] (Anderson, 2001; Horn, 2003) come to light in the interviews with alumni. The nature of these educational elements suggest processes or methods of teaching that may be transferable to other doctoral programs. A third way that this research may prove to be significant is in gleaning insight from the education of OD doctoral students that may be used in training OD professionals in a broader context outside of higher education. In addition, this work provides insight for current and future doctoral students to help them navigate their own educational process by seeing the big picture from the perspectives of both faculty and alumni. Last, this research provides well informed feedback to administrators and faculty of professional research doctorate programs from the alumni about their educational experience. This feedback could be used to advance both program and course development in universities that offer these types of degrees.

Mawhinney (2009) states, "The need to keep up-to-date with the business marketplace demands for professional knowledge, skills, and abilities is critical to the success of any higher education business program" (p. 13). Professional research doctoral programs that emphasize OD provide a strong link to the future of the field. As such, educational institutions would be wise to closely listen to the feedback from the influential group of people within this research study.

This volume is divided into three parts. Part I looks at some of the background literature that supports and informs the research project. The second part of the book explores the important findings from the study. Part III discusses the implications of these findings for the field of OD and the field of doctoral education.

NOTES

1. For an interesting treatment of "three generations of OD" see (Seo, Putnam, & Bartunek, 2004).
2. A professional research doctorate is one of three overarching categories of doctoral education (Gardner, 2009c). The other two are the research doctorate and the professional doctorate. The distinctions between these three types of doctorates will be explored below in Chapter 2.
3. Four professional research doctoral programs were chosen to participate in this study. Two of these are specifically identified as OD programs, one is a

doctorate in education and the other a doctorate of philosophy. In order to broaden the sample, the remaining two programs are both doctorates of management with strong organization development underpinnings. All four of these doctoral programs are listed in "The International Registry of Organization Development Professionals and Organization Development Handbook" (2010).

4. The following are some examples of the types of alumni perspective studies that do exist in the broader literature outside of OD.

    • In the arena of students' perceptions of the educational experience: MBA or business schools (Armstrong, 2007; Eidmann, 2002; Greene, 2007; Nash, 2002) and executive MBA education (Chrite, 1998; Hilgert, 1995).

    • Examples of alumni perspectives of doctoral programs specific to certain industries would include: hospital administration (DeVeau, 1994), pharmacy (Kelley, 2002), supply chain management (Mawhinney, 2009) and, science and engineering (Williamson, 2009).

Some examples exist of studies that look at the perceptions of doctoral programs by certain groups of people: historically Black colleges (Garrett, 2006), or female students (Leisure, 2007).

Some specific schools are highlighted as case studies. One example of this is a study of Saint Louis University's Educational Leadership Program (Everson, 2009).

The findings of many of these studies were particular to the industry, field, or personal characteristics of the participants and thus not directly transferable to the world of OD. In addition to the examples listed above, there are research studies that primarily look at the intrapersonal and interpersonal reflections of graduate school alumni on their educational experience. Two specific examples of this type of research are from Harris (2007) and Hilgert (1995). Harris (2007) found in her research that emerging themes of personal and professional life changes in doctoral programs included, "increasing personal capacity through changed understandings," "nurturing service to others through dialogue and building relationships," "recognizing the need for authentic leadership through responding to all learners," "becoming self aware through critical reflection," "spontaneous, informal mentoring by faculty, and other leaders," and that "the cohort itself consistently laid the foundation for growth to occur" (p. 331). The research of Hilgert (1995) on executive MBA alumni states that as a result of their educational experience they "valued themselves more as people," "placed a higher value on their time," grew in "self-confidence" and "self-acceptance," "broadened perspectives," and shifted from "role taker to role maker" (p. 71). The research findings of these studies focused on the internal landscape of the person; they are helpful in describing the personal development that can happen during graduate school. However, the lack of research on doctoral alumni perceptions of their educational experience in general, and more specifically in the field of OD points to the need for more studies in this area. Listening to alumni about their educational experiences is of prime importance and it is not effectively being done (C. Taylor, 2009).

5. Success for the graduate is defined here as finding a "rewarding position that offers legitimate opportunities for professional advancement" (C. Taylor, 2009, p. 48). Specific indicators of successful doctoral graduates will be explored from the view point of faculty in Chapter 4.

6. Hidden curriculum is "a broad category that includes all of the unrecognized and sometimes unintended knowledge, values, and beliefs that are part of the learning process in schools and classrooms" (Horn, 2003, p. 298).

PART I

BACKGROUND LITERATURE

Without any substantial body of knowledge on OD doctoral education, literature from the broader field of education provides background for this work and constitutes the three chapters of Part I. Chapter 2 explores literature on doctoral education. The topics of Chapter 2 include the historic purpose of doctoral education, descriptions of the three general types of doctoral education, and some of the current research on doctoral education. The third chapter specifically focuses on the doctoral student. The subject matter of Chapter 3 includes professional identity, transformative learning and professional development. Chapter 4 focuses briefly on adult learning and learning outcomes.

CHAPTER 2

DOCTORAL EDUCATION

During its long history, doctoral education has sought to prepare the next generation of scholars to produce generative knowledge within their chosen field of study (Gilbert, 2004). More recently the doctorate has been conceived of as the training ground for the *stewards of the discipline* (Golde & Walker, 2006, p. 5). Above all, a steward of the discipline is a scholar in the fullest sense of the term (Golde, 2006).[1]

THE PURPOSE OF DOCTORAL EDUCATION

A significant task during their doctoral studies is for students to develop an identity as a scholar and a member of a discipline (Austin & McDaniels, 2006). The salient purpose of doctoral education is "to educate and prepare those to whom we can entrust the vigor, quality, and integrity of the field" (Golde, 2006, p. 5). Generally speaking, doctoral education should prepare the steward for three specific tasks: (a) *creation of knowledge*, (b) *conservation of knowledge*, and (c) *transformation of knowledge* (pp. 9, 10). The first type of preparation entails learning to generate new knowledge that makes a unique contribution to the field. The full gamut of scholarship is in view here including asking interesting and important questions, formulating and conducting research, analyzing and evaluating the results, communicating the findings, and defending one's own knowledge claims against challenges and criticism of others (Golde, 2006). Second, the student should be able to critically conserve knowledge in the field. Conserving knowledge includes understanding the his-

Educating the Scholar Practitioner in Organization Development, pp. 11–16
Copyright © 2012 by Information Age Publishing
All rights of reproduction in any form reserved.

tory and foundational ideas of the discipline, balancing the depth and breadth of knowledge in the discipline, realizing how the specific discipline fits into the larger academic context, and discerning "which ideas are worth keeping and which have outlived their usefulness" (p. 10). The third way students should be prepared as stewards is to responsibly transform "knowledge that has been generated and conserved by explaining and connecting it to ideas from other fields" through writing, teaching and application (p. 10). Preparing the student for creation of knowledge is the most developed element of doctoral education (Golde, 2006). However, faculty members generally do not make explicit their "theories and strategies on the pedagogy of research for developing excellent researchers. Development of the skills, knowledge, habits, and abilities of conservation and transformation is even less systematic" (p. 14). The implication of this previous statement is that the pedagogy and process of developing stewards in their abilities to create, conserve, and transform knowledge needs to be deliberately thought through, articulated, and guided by faculty members.

Stewardship of the discipline also involves both a "set of roles and skills" as well as "a set of principles" (Golde, 2006, p. 9). Embodying the roles and skills of the discipline promotes competence, and embracing the principles provides ethical guidance for the scholar in the field (Golde, 2006). However, the specific formation of what it means to be steward is in some ways unique to each discipline of study (Golde, 2006). In short, development of scholars who will steward the advancement of a discipline is the purpose of doctoral education (Golde & Walker, 2006).

THREE TYPES OF DOCTORATES

As stated above the doctoral degree was originally designed to prepare students to be academic scholars and more recently thought of as developing stewards of the discipline (Golde & Walker, 2006). Nerad (2008) agrees that historically "the primary purpose and goal of doctoral education has been the preparation of the next generation of university professors who will become productive researchers and innovators, and in turn become teachers of the following generation" (p. 279). As such, the doctorate is the highest academic degree offered in the United States. Many different types of doctoral degrees exist; broadly speaking, they can be divided into three general categories. The three categories of doctoral degrees are (a) professional, (b) research, and (c) professional research (Gardner, 2009c). For sake of clarity, the focus of work is on the third type of doctoral program. All three categories of doctoral education will be briefly described below in order to place the professional research doctorate in its broader context.

The Professional Doctorate

The first general category of doctoral education is the professional doctorate. This type of doctoral program trains individuals who will work in "professional fields such as medicine, veterinary medicine, pharmacology, dentistry, psychology, and optometry" (Gardner, 2009c, p. 29). Professional doctoral degrees include MD., JD, and PsyD. In this type of degree a thesis or dissertation is usually not required; rather, these degrees "focus on training through lengthy internships and clinical experiences" (p. 30). Even though a formal thesis may not be required, professional doctorates have a strong research mindset and skill base undergirding them that is unique to each specific discipline.

The Research Doctorate

The research doctorate is the second type of doctoral degree. In a research doctorate degree program, academic research culminates in the form of a formal thesis or dissertation. The dissertation should demonstrate the production of original knowledge in order to advance the field of study. Research degrees include PhD, DFA, and ThD (Gardner, 2009c). Historically speaking, individuals who pursue this type of doctoral degree have been shaped toward being a career academic which involves research, writing, and teaching in their chosen field of study (Nerad, 2008).

The Professional Research Doctorate

The third type of doctoral degree awarded in the United States is the professional research doctorate. As the name implies, this type of doctorate combines a focus on both research and practice. A formal thesis or dissertation is usually required, and may be specifically geared toward investigating a particular professional topic or existing problem. Examples of professional research degrees are an EdD and the executive doctorate (Gardner, 2009c). Boud and Lee (2009) state these doctorates are "commonly profession-specific and are more directly aimed at mid-career professionals, or as advanced training grounds for particular professional groups" (p. 3). The emergence of profession-specific doctorates could be attributed to many factors, chief among them may be that prospective doctoral students, their employers, and other vested stakeholders do not believe the traditional research doctoral degree adequately prepares the graduate for the pressures and challenges of an advanced level, nonacademic, professional context (Gilbert, 2009; Usher, 2002). Indeed, "academia is no longer the dominant destination for doctoral graduates" (Gilbert, 2009, p. 55). Thus, the scope of doctoral education in the United States is expanding to include a broader array of educational programs to accommodate a wider range of professional needs. A continuum of options in doctoral education is emerging. The following section looks more closely at the research on the practice of doctoral education.

RESEARCH ON DOCTORAL EDUCATION

In recent years, research studying the practice of doctoral education has begun to look more closely at the effectiveness of the educational process (Boud & Lee, 2009). Whereas the number and range of studies on doctoral education are increasing, "knowledge is fragmented and partial" (Lee & Boud, 2009, p. 11). In the past, primary attention in research on doctoral education was paid to the production of research outputs, that is, the thesis or dissertation as the product of education (Boud & Lee, 2009). The historic goal of doctoral education has been to apprentice those who will work in the academy as scholars (Golde, 2008; Nerad, 2008). Consequently using the dissertation as the measure of educational success was appropriate. Postgraduate success was based on whether or not the individual obtained an academic position and tenure (Golde, 2006). Historically, doctoral curriculum has been largely shaped by the goal of fashioning the future academics of the discipline (Nerad, 2008). Within the framework of the research doctorate, the overarching focus remains on shaping scholars (Golde & Walker, 2006). However, with the advent of other forms of doctoral degrees that primarily educate practitioners, using the dissertation as the main or only source of evaluation may be shortsighted or not even applicable in some cases (i.e., the professional doctorate).

The landscape of doctoral education is changing. During the past decade a shift in focus is also beginning to take place in how doctoral education is researched. In fact the research studies investigating doctoral education are undergoing a significant transitional phase (Green, 2009). Rather than focusing on the formal thesis or dissertation as the product of doctoral education, current research studying doctoral education is exploring the practices involved in doing doctoral work and producing doctoral graduates (Lee & Boud, 2009). In other words, the most recent research on doctoral education is investigating the practice of doctoral education and in doing so transfers attention toward the doctoral student as the product of the educational process, rather than the primary focus being the dissertation document as the sole educational outcome (Boud & Lee, 2009). Both the graduate and the dissertation are being viewed as products of doctoral education. More specifically, the current research on doctoral education is explicitly examining "the graduate as the 'knowing subject' of doctoral work" (Lee & Boud, 2009, p. 19). The graduate "needs to be a certain kind of knower and a certain kind of self: research-capable, reflexive and flexible, with 'generic' as well as discipline—or field-specific knowledges and capabilities" (p. 19). The interest in doctoral students developing generic knowledge and skills "has been motivated by the belief that there are skills which all graduates should possess, and which would be applicable to a wide range of tasks and contexts beyond the university setting" (Gilbert, Balatti, Turner, & Whitehouse, 2004, p. 375). Reforming and updating the research component of doctoral education is what is in view, not replacing it (Prewitt, 2009).

Traditional research doctorates have primarily focused on Mode 1 academic disciplinary knowledge (Gibbons et al., 1994; Usher, 2002). In addition to Mode 1 knowledge, professional research doctorates also focus on Mode 2 transdisciplinary knowledge or that which is created in the context of application (Gibbons et al., 1994; Lee & Boud, 2009; Usher, 2002). Professional research doctorates explore Mode 2 knowledge making a strong emphasis on links between theory and practice. The ability to link theory and practice requires people who can operate in both realms. Students and graduates of professional research doctorates are poised to make these types of theory-practice linkages due to their professional backgrounds and their new found research skills and experience as doctoral students. In essence, professional research doctorate programs are seeking to develop *scholar practitioners*,[2] those who are more likely to bridge the theory practice gap (Huff & Huff, 2001). Understanding the theory practice gap and the role of the scholar practitioner as an individual who might help address the theory practice gap is relevant to the practice of the professional research doctorate. Chapter 3 focuses on the scholar practitioner doctoral student.

NOTES

1. Reframing the purpose of doctoral education to be stewardship of the discipline allows for a broader expression of career choices postgraduation other than tenure track faculty positions.

2. The literature uses the terms *scholar-practitioner* and *practitioner-scholar.* Both of these terms broadly speak to the same idea, a person who concurrently contributes to the field through research that leads to knowledge generation and through active effective practice in the field. The term scholar-practitioner will be used throughout this document merely for the sake of consistency and clarity.

CHAPTER 3

THE DOCTORAL STUDENT

Many fields of study in the social sciences struggle with a gap between academic theory and professional practice. Understanding the relationship between theory and practice has been the focus of professional research schools in psychology, "business, engineering, social work, medicine, agriculture, education, public administration, journalism and law" (Van de Ven & Johnson, 2006, p. 802). The disconnect between theory and practice has been broached many times; however, the gap largely remains as the "values and aims of science and practice are often experienced as antagonistic" (Pasmore, Stymne, Shani, Mohrman, & Adler, 2008, p. 13). Academics and practitioners dwell in different types of cultures, respect different types of expert knowledge, have different end products in mind, and in essence speak different languages. It is not surprising that a gap exists between the two worlds. One avenue by which it has been suggested that the theory-practice gap may be addressed is through the contributions of the scholar-practitioner (Hay, 2003; Huff & Huff, 2001).

Scholar-practitioners are *boundary spanners* (Huff & Huff, 2001, p. S50), who have one foot in the world of the academy and one foot in the world of practice. Advancing the causes of both theory and practice is their main concern (Tenkasi & Hay, 2008). These individuals "identify with the primary tasks of generating new knowledge and improving practice" (Wasserman & Kram, 2009, p. 12). Scholar-practitioners use expert knowledge drawn from both theory and experience to inform research, decision making, and action in the field. Since they understand the values and speak the language of both the academic and the practitioner,

Educating the Scholar Practitioner in Organization Development, pp. 17–24
Copyright © 2012 by Information Age Publishing

scholar-practitioners are likely to be the individuals who will help bridge or "potentially close the relevance gap from both ends" (Huff & Huff, 2001, p. S50).

Given the potential contribution of the scholar-practitioner, it is important to understand as much as possible what factors might contribute to the professional identity and development of these individuals, especially as it relates to the topic of the development of professional research doctoral students.

PROFESSIONAL IDENTITY

Broadly speaking, the bulk of research on professional identity has been dedicated to domain-specific areas of practice. For example, occupational therapists have specifically studied the professional identity of their own therapists; however this research has limited generalizability to other professional fields. A small amount of research has been conducted on the overarching phenomena of professional identity (Jebril, 2008). The salient concepts from the general literature on professional identity will be delineated below in order to provide a beginning framework. In addition, the notion of professional identity and the doctoral student is explored.

Understanding Professional Identity

Ibarra (1999) defines *professional identity* as "the relatively stable and enduring constellation of attributes, beliefs, values, motives, and experiences in terms of which people define themselves in a professional role" (p. 764). Findings from the research of Jebril (2008) suggest that professional identity is developmental, evolves throughout one's life, and is highly correlated with personal identity. In other words, professional identity develops over time as a "component of the experiential and maturation processes" of an individual (p. 20).

Professional identity is "culturally ascribed" (Jebril, 2008, p. 36). Socialization is a strong factor contributing to professional identity formation. Diverse experiences and meaningful feedback from coworkers help people gain insight about themselves and their specific professional preferences (Ibarra, 1999). The process of socialization encourages a person to internalize characteristics, values, attributes, and knowledge of a profession, as well as develop skills that contribute to a new professional self (O'Meara, 2008). As part of the socializing process, individuals within a professional culture tend to project a certain image that conveys "the qualities prescribed by their profession, such as competence, judgment, and trustworthiness, with the hopes that others will ascribe those same qualities to them" (Sweitzer, 2008, p. 47). The process of socialization plays a strong role in the development of professional identity.

Achieving professional status within a chosen field is another influential factor in professional identity development. Jebril (2008) notes that the components that build professional status include mastering "a set of philosophical assumptions, a systematic body of knowledge, a code of ethics, a domain of concern, aspects of practice" (p. 35) and the use of "legitimate tools" (p. 2). Negative effect on professional status happens through "professional role ambiguity, role erosion, role extension, and unclear definition for a profession" (p. 36).

Professional Identity and the Doctoral Student

Jebril (2008) found that professional identity is formed through experience and also through education. Advanced degrees and specialization in a particular field enhance the individual's sense of professional identity (Jebril, 2008). Part of the professional learning that takes place within advanced educational degrees is the specific processes of socialization that are unique to each field of study. In other words, socialization of students into a discipline is customary in doctoral education (Gardner & Mendoza, 2010). Socialization in graduate education affects how doctoral students see themselves, their work, what work is deemed valuable, and what it means to be a professional in their field (O'Meara, 2008).

Alongside of being a practitioner, a significant task for a doctoral student is to develop an identity as a scholar and a member of a discipline (Austin & McDaniels, 2006). To that end, one important aspect of doctoral education is the process of identity formation, which involves transforming one's identity from experienced professional to that of a researcher (Thomson & Walker, 2010). Thus, one way of "rethinking the work of doctoral education" is in facilitating the identity shift "from professional to researcher-as-professional" (p. 19). For some doctoral students, developing an identity as a researcher as well as maintaining an identity as an experienced practitioner results in an intense struggle to integrate these multiple identities. The observation has been made that, "most doctoral students face disjunctures between their sense of self as an adult, their placement as a novice in an expert scholar community, and their development of this new identity as a scholar and knowledge creator" (Kasworm & Bowles, 2010, p. 225). Educating doctoral students to find "synergistic connections" between their multiple identities "is a way of 'reprofessionalizing' academic work, one student at a time" (Colbeck,

2008, p. 14). One avenue by which faculty could help students with identity integration is for faculty to openly share their own evolution through professional identity integration (Colbeck, 2008). In addition, apprenticeship is an important part of socialization and identity formation in doctoral studies (Gardner, 2009a; Golde & Walker, 2006; Nerad & Heggelund, 2008). Doctoral students who are involved with "engaged professors" develop "a professional orientation that encourages connecting knowledge with real-world problems" (O'Meara, 2008, p. 36).

Gardner (2009b) states that "development at any level occurs as a result of two conditions: challenge and support" (p. 7). This is especially true of professional identity development during doctoral studies. Alongside of the research on professional identity, the literature on transformative learning and professional development also provides useful information that sheds light on developing the doctoral student.

TRANSFORMATIVE LEARNING AND PROFESSIONAL DEVELOPMENT

Transformative learning "provides a helpful framework for understanding the difficult process of doctoral students transitions, and forming and re-forming role identities and involvements" (Kasworm & Bowles, 2010, p. 230). While there is some research on this topic with undergraduate students, according to Kasworm and Bowles, there is no research that has focused upon transformative learning in the doctoral experience.

In this section, transformative learning will be looked at from three different vantage points. The first segment provides a basic understanding of transformative learning theory. The confluence of transformative learning and professional development is explored in the second segment. Last, the notion of transformative learning and the doctoral student will be addressed.

Transformative Learning Theory

People hold assumptions and interpretations about the world and their experiences in the world, and when these assumptions are sufficiently challenged, then a new or revised interpretation may be adopted and used to guide future action (E. W. Taylor, 2008). Generally speaking, these shifts in assumptions and interpretations about the world and the resulting actions are at the heart of transformative learning theory. Mezirow's (1991, 2000) *transformative learning theory* focuses on how adults learn, how they make sense of their experiences, how their perspectives about their experiences are transformed, and how this transformation affects their lives. The learning cycle of transformation generally follows some variation of the following phases:

(1) A disorienting dilemma, (2) Self-examination with feelings of fear, anger, guilt or shame, (3) A critical assessment of assumptions, (4) Recognition that one's discontent and the process of transformation are shared, (5) Exploration of options for new roles, relationships, and actions, (6) Planning a course of action, (7) Acquiring knowledge and skills for implementing one's plans, (8) Provisional trying of new roles, (9) Building competence and self-confidence in new roles and relationships, (10) A reintegration into one's life on the basis of conditions dictated by one's new perspective. (Mezirow, 2000, p. 22)

In simple terms, transformative learning happens through *perspective transformation* (Mezirow, 1991). Perspective transformation is a "process of becoming critically aware of how and why our assumptions have come to constrain the way we perceive, understand, and feel about our world" (p. 67). In addition to awareness of constraining assumptions, perspective transformation also involves the willingness to step out beyond these constraining ways of thinking by constructing and appropriating new ways of interpreting the world that are more fully developed and functionally effective. People become open to the possibility that the way they have interpreted and made meaning of the world no longer accounts for what they find to be true about their experience. Once an individual becomes aware of the constraining assumptions, it becomes possible to create "a more inclusive, discriminating, and integrative perspective" (p. 167). When a new perspective has been gained, then a choice to internalize this new understanding can be made and acted upon.

Perspectives are transformed through changes in *frames of reference* (Mezirow, 1991). Frames of reference are

structures of assumptions and expectations that frame an individual's tacit points of view and influence their thinking, beliefs, and actions. It is the revision of a frame of reference in concert with reflection on experience that is addressed by the theory of perspective transformation—a paradigmatic shift. (E. W. Taylor, 2008, p. 5)

Perspective transformation leads to a more developed and functional frame of reference, "one that is more (a) inclusive, (b) differentiating, (c) permeable, (d) critically reflective, and (e) integrative of experience" (Mezirow, 1996, p. 163). Transformative learning takes place when people open up and become aware of their frames of reference, discard obsolete ways of thinking, create alternative ways of seeing things, and act differently based on those new insights (Cranton & King, 2003). Simply put, "Transformative learning has to do with making meaning out of experiences and questioning assumptions based on prior experience" (Cranton, 2006, p. 8). The following segment explores the intersection of professional development and transformative learning.

Professional Development and Transformative Learning

When applied to professional development, transformative learning takes place when individuals critically examine their practice and acquire alternative ways of understanding what they do (Cranton & King, 2003). Meaningful professional development will go beyond the effective use of new tools and involve the entire person as a professional, including his or her beliefs and values (Cranton & King, 2003).

At least three factors promote professional development: individuation, authenticity, and transformative learning (Cranton & King, 2003). The notion of *individuation* entails the development of the whole person as a unique and distinct professional (Cranton & King, 2003). Without individuation there is "no foundation on which to question assumptions and norms" of the general populace, since the person does not see themselves as separate from those norms (p. 34).

The second factor that promotes professional development is *authenticity*. Authenticity is essential for professional development since it is "the expression of the genuine self in the community" (Cranton & King, 2003, p. 34). In other words, one's unique professional identity is being lived out for others to see.

Finally, transformative learning is necessary for professional development, as it brings to the surface underlying assumptions that may need to change in order for growth to take place. Critical self-reflection is an avenue by which assumptions are unearthed. Cranton and King (2003) state that "critical self-reflection" is a starting point "for continuing, self-directed professional development" (p. 35). Mezirow (1991) believes that "reflection is the process of critically assessing the content, process, or premise(s) of our efforts to interpret and give meaning to an experience" (p. 104). Surfacing and attempting to understand the tacit assumptions about one's self and one's work is what is in view here. Applying this reflective element to the workplace, Donald Schön (1983) speaks about the art of being a "reflective practitioner." Schön states,

> A practitioner's reflection can serve as a corrective to over-learning. Through reflection, he can surface and criticize the tacit understandings that have grown up and around the repetitive experiences of a specialized practice, and can make new sense of the situations of uncertainty or unique-

ness which he may allow himself to experience.... When a practitioner reflects in and on his practice, the possible objects of his reflection are as varied as the kinds of phenomena before him.... He may reflect on the tacit norms and appreciations which underlie a judgment, or on the strategies and theories implicit in a pattern of behavior. He may reflect on the feeling for a situation which has led him to adopt a particular course of action, on the way in which he has framed the problem he is trying to solve, or on the role he has constructed for himself within a larger institutional context. (pp. 61-62)

Critical reflection and transformative learning fit hand-in-glove with the art of being a reflective practitioner. Schön (1983) speaks about the manager's own actions as a reflective practitioner and speculates as to why this is difficult to develop in others within a work setting. Schön states,

> Managers do reflect-in-action, but they seldom reflect on their reflection-in-action. Hence this crucially important dimension of their art tends to remain private and inaccessible to others. Moreover, because awareness of one's intuitive thinking usually grows out of practice in articulating it to others, managers often have little access to their own reflection-in-action.... And it prevents the manager from helping others in his organization to learn to do what he can do. Since he cannot describe his reflection-in-action, he cannot teach others to do it. If they acquire the capacity for it, they do so by contagion. Yet one of a manager's most important functions is the education of his subordinates. (p. 243)

Gaining the ability to be a reflective practitioner and also teach others this ability is one of the more important roles of a manager according to Schön. One of the reasons that this ability is crucial is that it helps a person to make intuitive judgments or *reflection-in-action* that do not rely on technical analytical *knowing-in-action* (Schön, 1987). Broadly speaking, while reflection-in-action is the art of management, knowing-in-action is the science. Both of these sets of abilities are needed to be a good manager; however, critical reflection is at the heart of transformative learning in professional development. The following section looks at transformative learning and the doctoral student.

Transformative Learning and the Doctoral Student

Transformative learning provides a plausible schema for understanding the experiences of the doctoral student. Doctoral education has the capacity to transform a student's perspective in many different dimensions. For example, alongside of being a practitioner, a significant task for a professional research doctoral student is to develop an identity as a scholar and member of a discipline (Austin & McDaniels, 2006). To that end, one important aspect of doctoral education is the process of identity formation, which allows an experienced, highly skilled professional to transform into a researcher (Thomson & Walker, 2010). An identity shift takes place "from professional to researcher-as-professional" (p. 19).

Doctoral education has many challenges and pressures that are inherent in the process. Doctoral students participate in "a highly stylized, demanding, and competitive environment" (Kasworm & Bowles, 2010, p. 232). They experience life-changing events that influence their view of themselves and the world. Kasworm and Bowles argue that doctoral students experience disorienting dilemmas from all sides. For the doctoral student, disorienting dilemmas may take the form of internal conflict with multiple professional identities, or pressure to be socialized into the academy, and perhaps considerable pressure for "personal change, and the risk of losses of the self" (p. 233). When two identities with contrasting meanings and expectations are vying for attention, the individual student is likely to experience stress as a result (Colbeck, 2008).

For doctoral students, "integrating all the professional identities" is an important process to enhance their "productivity, time and energy management, and well-being" (Colbeck, 2008, p. 13). Colbeck observes, "Once an individual has accepted and internalized expectation for a role as part of his or her identity, that identity becomes a cognitive framework for interpreting new experiences" (p. 10). In transformative learning, adults "emotionally and cognitively experience a transformational process modifying their sense of themselves and their meaning within their other identities and worlds, of forming and more often transforming their sense of self and social identities" (Kasworm & Bowles, 2010, p. 231).

The educational goal of transformative learning is to enable adults to become independent and self-directed learners capable of finding their own understanding of reality through critical reflection (Weinski, 2006). For doctoral faculty, the challenge "is to recognize and aid the transformation of adults as they face disorienting dilemmas to their personhood and their beliefs" (Kasworm & Bowles, 2010, p. 233). Transformative learning theory provides a framework for helping faculty understand the pressures that are being exerted on doctoral students and offer a way forward in helping students navigate the discernment process of making sense of the newly emerging scholar identity that is forming throughout their educational process.

Overall, the goal of doctoral education is "to prepare professionals who integrate knowledge, skills, and values into one competent whole person" (Golde, 2008, p. 21). Having a mindset to help students learn is an essential aspect of being an effective faculty member. To that end, the chapter explores some of the precedent literature on adult learning and learning outcomes.

CHAPTER 4

ACHIEVING LEARNING

Each adult learner brings unique experiences, knowledge, attitudes, and skills. The educator challenges and supports the student to stretch and grow in individual and authentic ways, yet all the while intentionally socializing the student into the field of study. Simply stated, adult education is about learning. Chapter 4 focuses on the idea of achieving learning by briefly looking at two areas of study: adult learning and learning outcomes.

ADULT LEARNING

The field of adult learning is both broad and deep. Performing a comprehensive review of this body of literature is outside the scope of this work. However, three themes in the adult learning literature will be briefly touched upon as they are pertinent to the topic at hand. One theme from the adult learning literature is the promotion of a *learner-oriented* environment as opposed to a *teacher-oriented* environment (Brookfield, 2005; Brookfield & Preskill, 1999; Freire, 1997; Knowles, 1988; Schön, 1987; Vella, 1995). The educational paradigm of modernity was primarily a teacher-oriented schema (Colwill, 2005). The goals and agenda of education revolved around what the professor deemed as important content for students to know. Educational philosophy is moving away from the *banking approach* to education where teachers are seen as authorities who make deposits of content into the student (Freire, 1997). A learner-centered approach to education seeks to promote a dialogue between the students

---

Educating the Scholar Practitioner in Organization Development, pp. 25–29
Copyright © 2012 by Information Age Publishing

and their backgrounds, experiences, and interests; the professor who is a content expert and a facilitator of discussion; and the bodies of knowledge and effective practice in the field of study. In short, "a focus on learning would adopt the student's way of organizing knowledge and probably be less discipline defined and more problem-centered and contextually defined" (Boyatzis, Cowen, & Kolb, 1995, p. 10). The experience base of students, their identity, and "their thoughts about the relevance of their study program" all affect the way in which they learn (Nygaard, Holtham, & Courtney, 2009, p. 21). Students are more engaged if they believe that the coursework has relevance to their lives and workplaces (Knowles, 1988; Vella, 2004).

If education is to be learner centered, then students are intentionally made more responsible for their own learning. A second theme from the literature is advocating self-directed learning for adult learners (Brookfield, 1990; Knowles, 1988; Vella, 1994). Kasworm and Bowles (2010) state, "One of the hallmarks of success" of doctoral education "is doctoral students' abilities and actions to be self-directed learners: being able to pursue learning beyond their mentors, engaging in critically reflective examination of knowledge and disciplinary assumptions, and to become peer scholars to their doctoral mentors" (p. 225). In short, "current learning theory suggests that the key skills and attitudes of self-directed learning are pivotal for the success of adults in doctoral studies" (p. 226). Learning how to learn is the key task in becoming a self-directed learner.

Being a self-directed learner sets the student up to be a graduate who deliberately pursues learning the rest of his or her life. The third theme gleaned from adult learning theory is lifelong learning (Brookfield, Kalliath, & Laiken, 2006; Palmer, 1998). One way of "rethinking the work of doctoral education" is in terms of lifelong learning (Thomson & Walker, 2010, p. 19). Taking lifelong learning as a "starting point means that the doctoral degree ought to be a preparation for learning beyond the award itself and for what is offered and what is learnt through undertaking doctoral study" (Walker & Thomson, 2010, p. 22). In pursuing a posture of a lifelong learner, the constant influx of new ideas, theories, and practices keep a person up-to-date in a field of study. In addition, lifelong learners have the opportunity to be mentors of learning for others regardless of the context, whether they are in the academy or the broader professional world.

The field of adult learning has much more to say about how to create a learning environment that is ripe for adults to grow. The three elements mentioned above are bare essentials for effective adult education. Continuing to focus on the achievement of learning, the remainder of this chapter highlights some of the literature on learning outcomes.

LEARNING OUTCOMES

The study and use of learning outcomes is steadily growing. However, little is published in the area of doctoral education learning outcomes and even less on learning outcomes within the field of OD.[1] This section of Chapter 4 builds a beginning understanding of learning outcomes and looks at the intersection of learning outcomes and higher education.

Understanding Learning Outcomes

Learning outcomes have been defined as "any visible, measurable, behavioral or intellectual" factors that the faculty "expected to result" from the students participating in the educational program (Chrite, 1998, p. 76). The use of the term learning outcome

> reflects a conceptual shift towards making learning more meaningful and effective for students. It mostly refers to the qualitative outcomes of student learning which emphasize understanding and obtaining meaning rather than quantitative outcomes of learning which have a focus on acquisition of factual knowledge. (Varnava-Marouchou, 2009, p. 98)

Broadly speaking, Hussey and Smith (2008) name three "unit of activity" levels in which the term *learning outcomes* is used in the educational literature: (a) at the "teaching event level," (b) at the "modular or course level," and (c) at the "whole program level" (p. 108). To date, the most effective use of learning outcomes is at the teaching-event level, followed by course level, and poorly used at the programmatic level (Hussey & Smith, 2008). However, Hubball and Gold (2007) state, "Program-level learning outcomes are a central component of learning-centered curricula" (p. 7). Informing students as to what they can expect to achieve is a primary reason for program-level learning outcomes. As a result of these learning outcomes, students are better able to "organize their time and efforts, prepare for assessment, and see the links between and among segments of a curriculum, thus enhancing transferability of learnings" (p. 9).

Learning Outcomes and Higher Education

At this point in time, learning outcomes are localized phenomena, meaning each doctoral program must articulate its own. Since there is no single implementation strategy to developing curriculum that will accommodate all academic programs, "developing, implementing, and evaluating learning-centered curricula is thus a scholarly process" (Hubball &

Gold, 2007, p. 9). Each institution or field of study has the responsibility to research and implement its own learning outcome agenda.

Though it seems obvious, when defining learning outcomes, the needs of the learner are the starting point (George, 2009). Alignment must exist between the "kind of learning outcomes you are aiming for and the way in which you support and help the corresponding learning development" (p. 172). Some of the more general types of learning outcomes named in the literature are listed below:

- Attainments or measures of basic competence (James & Brown, 2005)
- Understanding ideas, concepts, and processes (Bourner, 1997; James & Brown, 2005)
- Cognitive and creative construction of meaning and generation of ideas (Bourner, 1997; James & Brown, 2005)
- Effective practice, i.e., how to practice, manipulate, behave, engage in processes or systems (James & Brown, 2005)
- Higher-order learning and the use of critical faculties, i.e., advanced thinking, reasoning, or metacognition (Bourner, 1997; James & Brown, 2005)
- Planning and managing one's own learning (Bourner, 1997)
- Dispositions, i.e., attitudes, perceptions, motivations (James & Brown, 2005)
- Personal development (Bourner, 1997; Gilbert, 2009)
- Membership, inclusion, self-worth—these reflect the learners' affinity toward, readiness to participate in, and sense of worthwhile contribution to the group where the learning takes place. It is concerned with establishing social and substantive identities in ways that reinforce the inclination to learn (James & Brown, 2005, pp. 10-11).

Gilbert (2009) outlines several learning outcomes aimed at doctoral students: "Original contribution (new facts or knowledge, formulating theories, reinterpreting data or ideas)," "Implementing research project," "Critical review of literature of field," "Methodological techniques and skills," "Independent critical thought," "Relevance to scholarship in the field," "Formulating problems," "Research ethics," "Personal development," and "Commercialization and acquiring grants" (p. 61).

Learning outcomes can be specifically defined, but faculty also need to be responsive, flexible, and alert to the actual needs of the current students (George, 2009). Overall, the principle in practice of higher education is to "evaluate our teaching methods against the learning outcomes that we are seeking for our students" (Bourner, 1997, p. 345). Developing learning outcomes that guide significant learning experiences is important work for doctoral faculty. Students will benefit from the careful attention given up front by professors who engage the student and the subject matter in deliberate and meaningful ways.

Part I has looked at the precedent literature that supports the research project. The second chapter explored some of the current research on doctoral education. Chapter 3 focused on doctoral students, and Chapter 4 briefly looked at literature pertaining to adult learning and learning outcomes. Part II focuses on the research findings.

NOTE

1. According to Kretovics (1999), "little research has been published regarding the learning outcomes of graduate business students" (p. 126). A more recent study stated that "schools of business are beginning to conduct outcomes assessments to determine the degree to which the goals of the schools and its constituents are being met, but little of this has resulted in published research on graduate business learning outcomes" (Armstrong, 2007, p. 62). Williamson (2009) argues that there is a need to measure outcomes of doctoral programs, but there are no common agreed-upon measures. Before the mid-1980s, very few institutions in higher education used outcome assessments (Kretovics, 1998). The "lack of a uniform definition of outcomes assessment has led many practitioners to instead define the purpose of outcomes assessment and leave the definition of the process to the individual institutions" (p. 29). Purpose statements talk about "collecting data" or "evaluation" but do not state the means by which these evaluations should take place (p. 29). The American Assembly of Colleges and Schools of Business guidelines do not specify what outcome "measures must be taken nor do they instruct the colleges as to methodology or process. Those issues are to be determined by the college faculty" (p. 4). Left to their own devices, each university must fashion its own processes by which to measure learning outcomes. Student course evaluations are used, but not many universities use overall program evaluations, exit interviews, or surveys of graduates (Armstrong, 2007). Williamson (2009) states that due to the lack of data from doctoral alumni, graduate school "programs return to examining the same established data points of program quality with no clearer understanding of what makes their programs effective or ineffective ... when the compass for the future of their doctoral programs lies directly in the hands of their graduate placements" (p. 227). Despite this lack of clarity on many fronts, conversations and research are moving forward in the area of learning outcomes in higher education.

PART II

RESEARCH FINDINGS

Part II looks at the research findings from the study upon which this book is based.

Chapter 5 explores the faculty members' perspectives and Chapter 6 examines the alumni perspectives. The seventh chapter synthesizes the findings of the research.

CHAPTER 5

FACULTY PERSPECTIVES

To reiterate, Chapter 5 reports the research findings that emerged from the interviews with 18 faculty members from four different doctoral programs. Three main sections describe the findings from faculty interviews regarding (a) the learning outcomes, (b) creating a learning environment, and (c) the indicators of successful alumni.

LEARNING OUTCOMES

The first main section of findings looks at the learning outcomes that the faculty desire for their students. The backdrop is the first research question: "What do doctoral faculty members identify as the most important learning outcomes for their students, and what is the nature of these learning outcomes?" Seven themes emerged from faculty interviews regarding learning outcomes: (a) knowledge of OD, (b) critical thinking, (c) research mindset and skills, (d) development of self, (e) being a change agent, (f) being a scholar practitioner, and (g) making a contribution to the field.[1]

Knowledge of the Field

The first learning outcome for doctoral students named by some of the faculty members was a clear understanding of the fundamentals of the field of OD. In one sense, this rudimentary learning outcome is a

Educating the Scholar Practitioner in Organization Development, pp. 33–63
Copyright © 2012 by Information Age Publishing
All rights of reproduction in any form reserved.

given, since all of the doctoral programs in this study either have OD as an emphasis or have a strong affiliation with the field of OD. However, several faculty members felt the need to state it, presumably, so as to not take it for granted due to its central importance. Faculty member (F4) stated,

> We want students to get a solid grounding in the fundamentals of organization development and change. So in the first year we have a bunch of courses that focus on that.... Another learning objective is to give them a real solid foundation in philosophy of science and organizational theory, and so we have a series of courses around that.

The previous statement underscores the commitment to dedicate a major part of the coursework in this particular program to understanding the fundamentals of the field of OD. Participant (F9) desires doctoral students to be "well-rounded" in their knowledge; they need to understand "most of the aspects of the field of OD." In addition, this same respondent (F9) stated that it is helpful for students to "have some sort of a conversation about what is the difference between OD, OB, org. change, etc." The reason respondent (F9) gave for the student to be aware of the other organizational sciences was so that the student will be "versed on the breadth of the fields." Faculty member (F15) argued,

> There is a field—there is a body of knowledge—actual bodies of knowledge related to OB/OD, and we don't expect them to be expert in all; but we want them to have some breadth of knowledge and then a feeling of expertise in a few deep areas. The areas can be their choice, but we want them to feel expert in a couple of areas when they leave.

The expectation of participant (F15) is clear that doctoral students need to be broadly conversant in their major field, but also have areas of special emphasis.

Critical Thinking

The ability to think critically was another essential learning outcome identified by doctoral faculty. Participant (F2) clearly stated the hope that doctoral students will learn

> how to think better. Definitely how to think better and how to stop and think, as opposed to reacting. How to have a better conceptual repertoire to respond to the world and to respond to situations that they face so that they have more than one way to interpret it, more than one way to make meaning

of it, different ways to think about it, and that they are not as quick to just react and do. I think that that makes for a thoughtful educated scholar.

The idea of having the patience and discipline to suspend one's own opinion about a topic or situation and then look at it from several different vantage points is what is in view here. Participant (F1) agreed by saying,

> We teach them to think critically—it is, in a way, to challenge everything that you hear and not challenge in a negative way, but to try to figure out the basic assumptions. And in transformative learning, we actually ask them to extend their frame of references and to represent different perspectives—it is not saying this is right or this is wrong.

In asking students to represent different perspectives on a topic or situation, implicitly they are expanding each graduate student's own view. Participant (F16) stated,

> What I am hoping for is that doctoral education will broaden their ways of thinking about their own practice so that their habitual ways of analyzing problems and defining problems and coming up with solutions and understanding how their organizations or classrooms or communities work—that those habitual ways of understanding those things will be challenged and broadened, and that students will realize there are multiple lenses and multiple frameworks that you can apply to understanding experience.

Faculty member (F10) used a metaphor to describe the idea of broadening the student's perspectives. Participant (F10) stated that students begin their studies,

> from the perspective of looking at life through a soda straw. There is a very narrow aperture of looking at life. And after you go through the doctoral program and you come out, you don't ever pick up that soda straw again because you realize that you need to think and act globally as opposed to thinking and acting individually. That is what I hope they take away. That's what I try to get them to realize when they complete my class and move on to the next. I want them to go with that aperture much wider open than when they began. When they began it was a soda straw; by the time they graduate, hopefully we've opened that aperture out to where they can look around and realize that there's a really big world out there that they can be a part of.

The ability to critically evaluate one's own habitual assumptions, analyze ideas from other people's perspectives, and broaden one's own perspective are the elements of critical thinking that were mentioned by faculty.

Research Mindset and Skills

Several interviews of the faculty members highlighted the importance of students understanding what quality research is as well as learning to perform acceptable research during their doctoral education. As an act of practice, rigorous research is likely to be a new phenomenon for many doctoral students. Participant (F14) spoke about helping students "to learn to be comfortable in the research world because that is something that for many of them is a new experience." While being comfortable with research is a first step, participant (F6) argued for doctoral students to deliberately venture into the research world. Faculty member (F6) stated,

> I hope they all learn to do basic research, to appreciate research, and to be able to read it intelligently. Even if they are not going to continue in academia, they need to be able to read the literature. Some of it is badly done, so they need to be able to read it intelligently. So if we are really training scholar-practitioners, for me that is critical.

The above quote draws attention to the skill of doing research, the attitude of appreciation for what constitutes excellent research, and the ability to critically evaluate the quality of research projects documented in the literature. Participant (F4) also stated the hope that students "learn how to do good, rigorous, high quality research whether it is quantitative or qualitative or some combination of the two" in whatever environment they find themselves, whether they are leaders, consultants, or professors. Clearly, the previous statement underscores the desire that students carry forward the research mindset and skills learned in their doctoral experience in order to responsibly put these research abilities into practice in their given contexts, whatever they might be.

Taking it one step further, faculty member (F15) argued that students should know "how to translate practical issues, problems, and opportunities into research questions so that they can do research that will make a contribution to practice." In the previous statement, there is a sense that this faculty member desires for students to proactively lean into research within their given context so that the research positively affects practice. Participant (F13) stated this in a slightly different way: "the *biggest* learning outcome is, can they produce some good research? Can they produce research that has both rigor and meaning?" The question focuses on the capability of doctoral students to produce rigorous research that has value and relevance in the world of practice. Then respondent (F13) immediately went on to say,

> And then secondly, are they able to inspire others in some of these new ideas that they are creating? ... Can you excite people? Can you, at the most

simplistic level—can you teach? Can you teach in a way that is transformative?

What is in view here is the ability to communicate the value of significant research that has the potential to impact others.

Finally, respondent (F18) underscored the desire for students to grow in their confidence regarding their ability to conduct research. In answering the interview question, "What are you most hopeful that students will learn from being in this program?" faculty member (F18) stated,

> Confidence is the one word. But you don't get confident unless you do good research. So what I am hopeful for is that students will do good research. But they get there collaboratively, making use of their committee—collaboratively but independently. We don't hand-hold, but clearly you want to be able to say, "I worked this through my committee" ... being a good researcher—it is like riding a bike, you never lose it.... You understand good research.

In other words, having walked through the rigorous process of research with the guidance of the faculty, students have the opportunity to grow in their confidence and their ability to conduct quality research. Apparently, the desire of this faculty member is that this confidence transfers with the doctoral student into their context as an alumnus; (F18) implied (through the use of the bike-riding metaphor) that one never loses the capacity of being a good researcher once it is confidently learned. Faculty member (F9) described this sense of authentic confidence in one's own research as "finding their own doctoral voice." An example of finding one's doctoral voice that respondent (F9) spoke about was when students or alumni write an article with confidence and clarity in such a manner that practitioners can read the article, understand it, and apply it "without it being dummied down."

In summary, with regard to research abilities, faculty members spoke about helping students to be comfortable with the research world, appreciating good research, the ability to read and stringently evaluate research literature, responsibly conducting and applying impactful research, developing confidence in one's research abilities by doing good research, and finding one's authentic doctoral voice.

Development of Self

Several faculty members explicitly named development of self as an important learning outcome for doctoral students. The hope of faculty member (F1) is that doctoral students will primarily learn "about them-selves," and to that end stated,

> Each class ends up with a reflection paper. We push them in every class to assess self ... we push self-reflection. They change over three years and as a faculty we notice the dramatic change in them. People become more reflective.

And yet respondent (F1) said, "Of course students need OD skills and knowing how to do research—anybody can learn skills. Personally, I place more emphasis on personal self-development." Professor (F1) drew the connection that self-reflection opens up the opportunity for personal development. Participant (F16) remarked about the importance of "critical reflection." When asked to describe the idea of critical reflection, faculty member (F16) stated, "It's the process by which we become aware of the assumptions that we operate under, the assumptions that frame our actions and decisions and judgments." Participant (F13) described an assignment given in class to promote reflection:

> I provoke as a first major assignment a personal vision statement. I want them to look at their core values. I want them to look at their operating phi-losophy. I want them to look at their fantasies. I want them to look at their passion, there sense of legacy, their calling. I want them to contemplate their noble purpose in life. I want them to think about their intellectual agenda. And then I push them into even considering their family relation-ships, their intimate relationships with their spouse or partner, or finding one if they don't have one. I want them contemplate their spiritual health, their physical health, their contributions to community.... Once you are into this kind of work in a doctoral program—it's transformative.

Faculty member (F13) described taking this assignment a step further:

> I then also try to provoke them into or talk them into having their spouses do the same exercise. So then it increases the likelihood that they are learn-ing how to do this personal visioning in a very comprehensive salient way. I think that is really important, because if stuff shows up and they don't really see this as the heart of the new self—the next great adventure of their lives—then they are going to be spending an awful lot of time and energy and money chasing something that they should not bother chasing. I can't make that call—they might have to.

The above assignments aim at helping students identify their unique per-sonal vision for the future and what type of impact they hope to have on their world. The terms "push" (F1) and "provoke" (F13) used above are strong words expressing the fervency and passion with which these faculty members desire to see students engage in self-reflection and development of self.

Participant (F14) stated that doctoral students need to be people who understand and exhibit a "high degree of emotional intelligence. I want people with a high degree of self-awareness ... being able to learn how to manage themselves effectively in all kinds of relationships." Faculty member (F14) drew out the implications of self-awareness in the workplace saying,

> I hope that they will learn about themselves and what their strengths and opportunities are for growth and the way that they use themselves in their roles as managers in the variety of kinds of organizations that are represented. I hope that they come away with an understanding of themselves that enables them to be caring, compassionate, and considerate of the people that look to them for direction and guidance. And with that insight, they are able to hear more clearly what the folks who are looking to them for that direction and guidance are trying to say to them ... that they understand themselves well enough that they can make appropriate choices as to how they would interact with others in the organization.

The above faculty member made the connection that the self-awareness of the student is linked to being caring, effective, and impactful in their work environments. In addition to being self-reflective, respondent (F16) spoke about empathetically reflecting on other people's perspectives. The desire of faculty member (F16) is

> to make students critically reflective about their practice. To be able to understand how power operates in every situation, which to me is at the heart of being critically reflective—to be able to use different lenses of experience, of colleagues perceptions, of research and theory, to look at the practice from the lens of the client's eyes. I think generally, the hope for me is that students will learn a habit of being critically reflective, constantly trying to understand what assumptions they are operating under and to look at those assumptions through different lenses.

The previous quote highlights the importance of being aware of one's own assumptions and suspending them in order to examine a situation or idea from different perspectives. Awareness of others and listening to other perspectives is implicit in this type of reflection.

Self-development was identified by faculty as an important learning outcome for doctoral students. Based on the interviews with faculty, the learning outcome of self-development entails self-assessment, the desire and capability to self-reflect, the ability to discern and articulate a unique personal vision, growth in emotional and social intelligence, and the ability to critically reflect on essential issues from other people's perspectives.

Change Agents

Being an agent of change is a role that some of the faculty explicitly desire for their students to embrace as alumni. Participant (F8) stated, "I emphasize that they see themselves as an agent of change; a person that is capable of leading or supporting change work and that be deeply grounded in a set of values that they are clearly conscious of." The previous statement points to skills and a set of internalized values needed to be an effective leader of change. Faculty member (F4) emphasized similar ideas:

> My hope is that they will become really skilled change agents in their organizations because about sixty to seventy percent of our students stay in industry or organizations of some sort. They continue to be leaders in those companies. Some of them are HR leaders, some are line leaders, some of them are chief financial officers; they really run the gamut. But they are people who end up being change agents in the organization, and so what I really want them to learn is how to do change really well in a way that is effective and successful in building the company and also honoring of people in their quest for meaning and growth and development and success.

The above quote points out the need for change-agent skills and humanistic values, but also the assumption that many of the students will be called upon to be change agents from within an organization rather than as a consultant brought in from outside. Respondent (F3) reiterated this idea in stating the desire for doctoral students to learn "how to be effective change agents. And when I say change agents, I am not talking about consultants alone. I am talking about anybody responsible for change in any organization, anywhere in the world, and any kind of organization." The notion of a change agent (whether as a leader or a consultant to an organization), according to the faculty interviews, involves the effective use of OD skills and a humanistic set of values.

Scholar-Practitioners

In addition to being change agents, the notion of being a scholar-practitioner was also named in faculty interviews as being an important learning outcome. Participant (F15) described the doctoral student, who is a "scholar-practitioner" as

> a polished OD practitioner and researcher simultaneously so they have relational skills, they would have emotional intelligence, they would know about how to design adult learning experiences, they would be well-versed in

quantitative and qualitative methods for research, and they would be good writers. And they would enjoy writing—they wouldn't find it threatening or tedious.

Several faculty members underscored that the intention of their doctoral programs was to develop scholar-practitioners or practitioner-scholars. For example, participant (F4) stated,

> I teach in a doctoral program in which all of our students are scholar-practitioners and most of them are full-time working managers and executives in companies doing fun and exciting work in their organizations. They are all very accomplished professionals, and so my job as a professor in the program is to connect them with the vast knowledge in terms of the best readings and the best research and the best scholars in the field and then to invite them to take that and apply that in their organizations and do additional research with it. So what I love about that is that we get to operate in the world of ideas. We are talking about concepts and ideas and theories and research, but then also how does that apply in practice. It is really like putting together puzzles that integrate theory and practice and go back and forth informing the two.

Preparing students to integrate theory and practice through performing research and applying the new knowledge in their organizations seems to be the main thrust of the above quote. Faculty member (F4) desires to produce "scholar-practitioners"; whereas participant (F5) stated the intention of developing "practitioner-scholars." Faculty member (F5) stated, "We want to turn out practitioner-scholars. We want to turn out people that will add to the literature in their field. That they can solve really knotty unsolvable problems, and they have got those skills to do it."

Professor (F12) designs coursework that tries "to bring in academic rigor and blend it with practice" in order to equip students for their future work. Participant (F2) stated that since the program is "a scholar-practitioner program" students,

> should be as equally aware of where their own skillsets and development needs are on the practice side or on the scholarship side. I wouldn't expect people to be one-hundred percent on both, but they should understand where their own room for growth is when they are leaving.

Participant (F5) described the expectations for alumni of the "practitioner-scholar" program:

> I want them to write. I want them to add to the field of knowledge, but they are not going to be publishing in Academy of Management Journals. They are going to be in *Practitioner,* they are going to be in *Training and Development,*

and they are going to be in management journals. So I see our graduates staying in their jobs, going up to senior-level positions, becoming an external consultant or internal consultant in the organization, teaching part-time probably adjunct at some university or college and least likely full-time tenure track. They could do it, but they would have to really justify what a practitioner degree would do for a tenure-track scholar—and some of our students have—but that is the minority.

Being change agents and scholar-practitioners were mentioned as two of the intended learning outcomes for which faculty desire students to embrace as students and eventually as alumni.

Contribution to the Field

The last learning outcome that faculty members specifically stated is their desire for doctoral students to make a contribution to the field. Faculty member (F11) succinctly stated,

What I am looking for is a person who has an ongoing sense of responsibility first of all to their own development, to their cohort, to the program and to the field—to be an ongoing contributor—somebody who is not only going to sustain but to build the culture of the program and contribute to the field.

The above statement paints an almost visual picture of concentric spheres around the individual doctoral student in which their contributing influence is felt. Faculty member (F4) stated a similar idea in saying,

I really want them to fall in love with the field of OD and be committed and excited about making a contribution to the advancement of the field so that other scholars and scholar-practitioners that come along after them will be able to stand on and build on their work.

The passion for the field of OD came through in the interviews with faculty members. They desire for students to know and love the field in order to make a significant contribution.

CREATING A LEARNING ENVIRONMENT

This section of findings flows out of research "How do doctoral faculty structure their programs to achieve these learning outcomes, and how are these learning outcomes assessed?" The title "Creating a Learning Environment" was chosen because the findings reported in this section have as their common theme the ways faculty spoke about how they tangibly helped students learn. The intentional structures, processes, and assessments that the faculty put in place for doctoral students to aid their learning is the essence of this second section. Seven themes surfaced in faculty interviews: (a) focusing on the individual student, (b) building on the student's experience base, (c) creating a collegial ethos, (d) the cohort model, (e) connecting to the profession, (f) exposure to leaders in the field, and (g) assessment of learning.

Focusing on the Individual Student

Several faculty members discussed the deliberate attention they devote to the individual needs of students. Participant (F15) stated,

> We do a lot of counseling, and their mentors work quite a bit with them, at least I do, trying to get them the sense of how they are going to make a contribution. So most of them would fit somewhere on the scholar-practitioner continuum, and I would say that most of them would be closer to the practitioner side.

The above faculty member attempts to listen and counsel individual students as to where their best fit might be and how they can make a contribution as alumni. Participant (F18) sees the unique trajectory of each student's life and tries to help them discover more about themselves through the educational process. Faculty member (F18) maintained that

> These are students who have careers, they have backgrounds; it became clear probably in the second or third year of my teaching that what we were really doing was we were helping to shape and mold people in the directions that they desired but on a path that we could call OD. The individual student came in unique and left unique. But there was an affinity for a core set of values that underpin our field. But how a person approaches that work, it became more and more clear to me, was very individualistic, and this has been true particularly in our last couple of classes.

The previous quote underscored the increasing realization on the part of faculty member (F18) that in creating a learning environment, one must respect the unique perspectives of the individual student, but also "shape and mold" students with regard to their chosen profession, and that faculty members exert some sort of influence in this shaping process. Participant (F6) suggested that "people come in with such different needs and goals. We are aiming to meet those needs and goals—whatever they are." Faculty member (F6) elaborated further: "So, if someone comes in wanting to improve their ability to work in OD [internal or external], coming out at the other end with that done means more skill, self-awareness, confidence, and thus better able to do the work." An illustration of this individual attention to students is demonstrated by professor (F6) in the quote below:

> F6: We really work hard to serve students well.
> Interviewer: Could you draw that out?
> F6: I can do it personally; I don't give up on people easily. I think of one person who came in and had no ability to be self-reflective; incredibly smart person with, I think, a photographic memory; an amazing person. She instantly turned off the cohort. I worked with her for nine months to a year as she had negative encounters with the other students. And I worked with her on reflection, and urged her into spiritual direction or therapy or something. She finally dropped out, but I put in hours and hours to see if she could be reflective enough to survive the cohort, not to mention OD.

Realizing that the student had rough edges that were clashing with the other members of the cohort, the faculty person knew this person would also probably struggle working in the field of OD. The hard work exhibited by this faculty member illustrates the importance of caring for the individual needs of students.

Building on the Student's Experience

In addition to being aware of the individual needs of students, a second way faculty focus on their students is in respecting and building on their student's experience base. Participant (F4) believes that doctoral students "are all accomplished professionals, all very bright, all have had lots of experience, and so you get to operate at a very high level with these folks because they are pushing the frontiers of knowledge—both theoretical and practical."

The respect that this faculty member has for the doctoral students and their professional experience is clear. Faculty member (F2) simply stated that doctoral students

> have interests of their own. That is, they are not exactly blank slates. They start with experience and they start with interest areas that they are pursuing so that whatever is being discussed can be developed through a lens, and you get reactions from people that are based a lot on their own interests.

This faculty person exhibited the awareness that students bring their own interests and experience base with them, and that this may affect their interactions in the classroom discussions. Beyond discussions in the classroom, faculty member (F2) went on to say,

> One strength of this doctoral program is the weaving together of work experience with new knowledge. I think a lot of the students attempt to do that, and I see it taking place—operationalizing a lot at our school. My sense has been that people come with strong work backgrounds.... There seems to be a high quality to the students at our school, and I connect that to their background and work experience.

The above quote highlighted this faculty member's observation and appreciation that due to their "strong work backgrounds," doctoral students should be encouraged to make connections between their work experience and the new knowledge they are gaining from being in the doctoral program. In short, the students' experience base is seen as a plus. Participant (F5) made a similar observation:

> Most of our students are experienced managers, so they come with problems like any client would if you were consulting. And most of them are either senior or very high middle management.... They ask hard questions. I can talk about theory and they will say, "Well, I have this problem and it is a real tough problem." *And it is*, so that I have to stop and think as if I am dealing with a consulting client rather than with a student.

This faculty member recognizes the advanced experience base of the doctoral students in this program and responds to the student's questions that surface in class in the way one would speak to a consulting client, with respect and professionalism. The questions that are posed by students become the focal point of discussion.

Creating a Collegial Ethos

The next theme mentioned by faculty was creating a collegial ethos. Participant (F4) specifically stated about doctoral education,

> I like the more collegial nature of the classrooms; it is pretty much seminars. You invite everyone to do all of the readings, and sometimes students have to come in prepared to present on some of the readings, but it really is dialogue around ideas rather than straight-up teaching or lecture or case studies.

This professor highlighted the seminar format of teaching that allows the students to study ahead of time and come to the class time prepared to dialogue with the professor and the other participants around the sub-ject matter. Faculty member (F4) took it one step further and stated that students "are, along with me, the creators of knowledge; rather than sim-ply consumers of already-packaged knowledge. That is something that you get to do at the doctoral level, which from my perspective is really cool."

Building an environment where students can be creators of knowledge and not "consumers of already-packaged knowledge" describes a collegial ethos. Students are treated as contributing and respected professionals. Faculty member (F16) pointed to the strong experience base of students as a reason for building a collegial environment. Participant (F16) main-tained,

> Doctoral students have a strong reservoir of experience, and so one of the most important lenses that you view literature through is the lens of your own experiences as a practitioner. So unlike preservice students who are training for the field, typically, doctoral students are relatively senior in their own fields of practice, and so they have this vast reservoir of experi-ence, which means that in a sense, you are talking to peers, which I really enjoy.

While this professor showed respect for the experience base of the stu-dents, participant (F16) also noted,

> You may, as a professor, have a stronger grasp of theoretical literature or research that is being conducted, but in many instances, the students have experiences that are different to your own or are deeper and longer than your own, and so that's one of the main pleasures of working at the doctoral level. You are basically working with a group of peers who are skilled practi-tioners with a lot of relevant experience.

Professor (F16) encourages students to share their knowledge due to their strong professional backgrounds; however it is clear that participant (F16) understands the responsibility of the professor to bring academic expertise to the classroom as well. Participant (F8) spoke about an assign-ment that helps students draw out and articulate their own "ethical core," and described the respectful manner in which the faculty members inter-acted with students,

> In my teaching, I put an emphasis on developing an ethical core that the person would frame as their set of beliefs, and the faculty know that we would all read their core ethical positions and then try to respond to them as individuals—not as much as neophytes or people who are just entering a new field—we felt more like these are already professionals that had an identity. How does this field enhance or how does it engage them and, very

importantly, how will they take the field forward rather than just replicating what we did? What will they be doing with this work?

Positive regard is shown for the doctoral students in encouraging them to develop their own "ethical core positions." The faculty members in this program interact with individual consideration of the students around this assignment, especially with regard to where it will lead them along the path of their own choosing. Even though participant (F8) challenges students with knowledge of the field, this faculty member does not necessarily want to push students into following the same path as the professors. Faculty members at this school are not assuming that students will desire to follow the same professional path as those who are currently the leaders of the field. Participant (F8) stated that the use of this assignment

> really shifted the teaching philosophy from a standard body of knowledge that somehow must be conveyed to a set of values that the students connect to, frame in their own way, and then move through that in terms of a sort of action orientation. How are they going to make this happen in a world that they live in that doesn't look much like anybody else's world necessarily. So from a philosophical perspective, what I think doctoral education is—what all education should be—is highly focused on the individual needs with a set of assumptions that the world of knowledge offers, but neither one in a sense of a priority setting they both are critical. It's not one or the other— it's not even sequencing one after the other—it is doing it simultaneously, attending to both.

This professor argued for a learning environment that affords the confluence of individual needs and student interests connecting to a body of knowledge that the field of OD offers.

The Cohort Model

The cohort model of doctoral education has been adopted by all of the programs that participated in this study. Participant (F9) spoke about the importance of having the students start off during their orientation time meeting together on campus in their cohorts. Respondent (F9) stated,

> I think that helps to deepen the learning, deepen the bonding of the students together. They are able to start their cohort in that time, which I think is *really* effective for getting them hitting the ground running pretty quickly, and the core faculty does an excellent job of explaining the parameters of the program ... they kind of lay out, "This is what we teach in year one, year two and year three; here are your expectations for your papers, et cetera.

Faculty member (F9) also highlighted the positive impact that meeting in the cohort groups has on the educational process. Other faculty members point to the cohort model of doctoral education as a significant contributing factor in the learning environment. Faculty member (F4) forthrightly stated that one of the strengths of the program

> is the cohort model, because all of these students go through the first two years together and then the third year, sometimes the fourth or fifth year, they work on their dissertation. The first two years, they are in class together in a cohort, so they are learning just as much from each other as learning from the visiting professors, as much as they are learning from the literature, and so it is a real great combination of learning experiences.

The observation that students greatly learn from their interactions with each other is highlighted in the previous statement. Faculty member (F16) took it a step further maintaining that in the cohorts,

> there is a lot of peer teaching and peer learning that happens so the faculty's responsibility is preliminarily to identify what some useful resources will be and to frame some important questions, and then the students do a lot of work online before they meet with faculty. We regularly comment on their responses to the questions that have been raised. And then we ask the student in the time we have with them basically to do peer teaching in the face-to-face sessions as well. So I think that in the online components and in face-to-face, it's essentially a discussion-based peer-teaching approach.

The element of "peer" teaching and learning seems to be at the heart of this program's cohort model. The responsibility of the faculty, according to participant (F16), is in providing resources, asking thought-provoking questions, and providing some guidance and critique of the interactive process. In describing the capstone doctoral class, faculty member (F16) stated,

> We don't really need to give very many lectures, although we are quite willing to give our two cents, or more than our two cents worth. But our working assumptions is that the students are also very capable of creating meaning themselves from these materials and sharing what those meanings are and critiquing the materials. So that is sort of the way that we run the class, that is, the peer-teaching approach.

The willingness on the part of this faculty member to add to the knowledge base and facilitate discussion, as well as trust that the students will be able to forge meaning in their interactions, is the import of this previous quote. The cohort model allows for faculty-facilitated discussion and a student-peer teaching and learning approach to doctoral education.

Connection to the Profession

In addition to the cohort model, another way that doctoral students build relationships, as well as become socialized into the field, is through the intentional effort of the faculty to help them make connections to the profession. Several faculty members spoke about the importance of being socialized into the field and making connections to the profession. From the start of the doctoral program, participant (F7) aims toward socializing students into the field. Faculty member (F7) stated,

> I think the fact that they come in asking, "What is this doctoral program all about? What do I have to know to get through this thing? What do I have to do?" I try to put their minds at ease. I try to give them some tools, some lessons learned.... I guess I find that very rewarding in that I see all of these people coming in all nervous and concerned about how to graduate, and I try to get them off on the right path. It is really socialization. Getting them to understand that you have got to start thinking about what excites you—what is your passion? To go through a doctoral program and not have something you are passionate about—you know it is going to be boring as ###. And you are probably not going to make it, frankly, if you don't find something that you are passionate about within the field.

Participant (F7) underscored the gradual socializing process of easing students into doctoral studies by answering initial questions and providing useful tools and lessons, then eventually helping them identify their passion areas within the field and ultimately make a contribution to the profession.

One avenue by which faculty encourage students to become connected to the field is through attending and presenting at academic and professional conferences. Faculty member (F4) stated that students are exhorted to be

> really focused on making a contribution to the field of organization development and change. All of our students are continuously presenting at conferences—the Academy of Management conferences and other conferences around the world. We are helping to advance the state of the art of the field as well as being an educational program.

The expectation is set that students will begin to be contributing members of the field before they graduate, and that this should carry on once they become alumni. The interaction with faculty member (F11) and the researcher underscores this idea of socializing students into the profession:

> F11:   The primary strategy and requirement on our part is to socialize students into the field. I would say that that is really number

> one. When you talk about what we try to do … it is a given that they need to know content, and it is a doctoral degree, and so they need to know research methodology. But they have to be socialized into the field … socialized into the field to the extent that it is a continuing part of their life. I think that that is the continuing challenge for us.

Interviewer: To follow up on that: do you have things in mind that you do to actively socialize them into the field?

R11:   Absolutely. That is a major part of the orientation session where we take them through the professional associations and the expectations. We alert them to if you are planning an academic career at some point in your future that these are the kinds of things that you need to be prepared for and so forth. And you might want to attend the doctoral consortiums at the Academy of Management, if that is what you aspire to. If you are going to stay in corporate, that is of secondary importance. We strongly encourage people to attend the business meetings at the Academy because that is really where you find out what is happening at the Academy. The orientation session is so full— but they don't remember it. If it makes some kind of minor impact, I think that we are lucky. But then we have to continue reinforcing that through making sure that they get on programs, that they are submitting papers, and that they are part of panels. We try to use the cohort because there are subgroups that tend to cluster together and reinforce each other. But that continues on for the entire three-year period.

The intentional socialization of students into the field is seen in the above interaction. From the very beginning of their doctoral education, students are rehearsed in the importance of attending and presenting at conferences as a way of building ongoing connections to the field. Faculty member (F2) made a similar observation:

> Most programs will encourage students to attend at conferences at least once while they are a student … our program is actually creating ways for more students to not only attend but actually engage in and present or get involved in the way the conferences run. Whether it is a regional or a national, it is partly the experience base and it's the connection. I think the emphasis is on connecting to the professional network. And I think that emphasis is pretty strong. And there are numerous schools that wouldn't pay any attention to that at all. Part of the impact of that is that people are much more integrated into the profession by the time they graduate.

Faculty member (F18) took this idea a step further and stated, "We actually make it required that they be at the Academy of Management; that every one of them publish or present or submit to a regional academic conference." The requirement to attend, present, or publish at an academic conference ensures participation in the broader network at least to some degree while the student is in the program; this seems to be the intent of the comment by faculty member (F18). Participant (F2) stated some additional ideas about students making a connection with one another. Faculty member (F2) stated,

> I think that one of the things that happens with doctoral education in general is this connection to the profession.... What happens to a lot of people, once they become more "scholar-practitioner-like"; I think automatically they grow a greater interest in a broader professional network and other people who have interesting ideas. Rather than run away from, you run towards other people with interesting ideas, and I think that happens faster after a doctorate than it does in other stages of life because that sense of inquiry that has been instilled a little bit more during the doctoral work.

Discussing interesting ideas with other scholar-practitioners leads to engagement with the broader network; this engagement seems to be ignited in doctoral education, according to the above statement. Participant (F2) stated that the "sense of inquiry" and discussion noted above leads people to more collaboration.

> It helps people to get out of the box of becoming too competitive, and it makes people become more interesting to each other and more collaborative with other people and more interested in finding out what makes things tick or what is driving somebody else's interest. I think that there is something there that is both a combination of how that inquiry carries forward but also the way it connects people to a broader professional community.

The sense of inquiry and investigation alongside of seeing the benefits of collaboration promotes student involvement with both cohort members and the broader community.

Exposure to Leaders in the Field

Deliberately using the cohort model of education and intentionally building connections to the broader professional community are two ways that doctoral faculty socialize students into the field. Another way that faculty members mentioned that they socialize the students to the broader field is through exposure to leading practitioners and academic thought leaders in the field. Faculty member (F11) maintained that

> It has always been a hallmark of the program to implement this concept of dialogue by bringing in the absolute best people in the field—the visiting

professors should be in every classroom. The anchor faculty is responsible for identifying them and bringing them in and giving the students the opportunity to dialogue with the absolute best. That is really what the program is all about.

Allowing the students to dialogue with faculty and practitioners exposes them to the broader field of OD. Faculty member (F4) agreed that

> one of the big ways that students are socialized into the field is that we bring in the ... recognized leaders in the field and so you know that what they bring in is going to be the very best and at the very leading edge of the field ... these are the leading minds in organizational change, organization development, strategy, leadership, et cetera. It is literally giving the students access to the people who are the pioneers and the leading edge of the field.

However, not only dialogue with these leaders of the field, but also this faculty member talked about "access," which hints at other points of collegial interaction besides classroom discussion. Building relationships among colleagues and promoting socialization in the field are both themes that emerged from the faculty interviews.

The intentional structures, processes, and assessments that the faculty put in place for doctoral students to aid their learning is the essence of this second section. The last theme that emerged from the interviews focused on the assessment of learning.

Assessment of Learning

Faculty members spoke about several ways that they assess learning in their doctoral programs. Reflective integrative, and practical assignments were talked about in addition to the dissertation project.

Reflective Integrative Assignments

One faculty member described in detail a way of evaluating and giving feedback on a student's work through a particular type of assignment in the doctoral program. Participant (F16) described this assignment, the capstone course's final paper, which is a "formal" paper but "not a typical paper" that looks at

> disembodied content and showing how that is understood. This paper is actually asking them to look back over their experiences in the doctoral program and to look at the ways the material they have studied has changed them or deepened their existing understanding of something, so the final

paper is more sort of reflective stock-taking of what the whole doctoral experience has meant for them. So that's something that we evaluate as probably the main piece of sustained work in the course.

Interviewer: How, if the paper is reflective, and then probably quite personal, how do you evaluate it?

F16:   Well, how we specifically evaluate these—what we are looking for—these are self-reported, so there is always, I think, some questions over self-reported descriptions of transformation.... We are trying to make sure that there is a clear inferential link between material that is in the program and the claims they are making around their own change and transformation. So if a student handed in a paper which basically said "Well, I changed this way and that way," but there was no connection to the program's activities or materials, then we would send the paper back and say what you need to do and we give very detailed feedback— "Show us here, here, here, and here specifically what it was within the program that caused this transformation." Or, if a transformation or change or influence is described in the paper; but we don't see that it has been very fully documented, then we will ask for more information. So you can't just say, "Well I read such and such and then I changed my practice." There has to be, I think, a deeper level of analysis. What was it about the original idea that caused you to focus in on this? Was it that it illuminated something you have been dealing with up to this time in your life, but not really understood properly and now this idea comes along that helps you understand it all? Or is it something else? So most of the feedback, I think we give on this, is just helping them more fully elaborate on the connections between their understanding of the materials that they have covered in the doctoral program and their own practice as change agents and consultants and practitioners.

The faculty member described guiding the students in reflection of their own journey through their doctoral studies, and how and why it affected them personally and professionally. The feedback provided by the faculty member in the above assignment was designed to help the students in the program progress in their abilities to critically reflect on their own life and practice. In addition to this example of an integrative reflective assignment, several faculty members also mentioned examples of practical assignments in their interviews.

Practical Assignments

Practical assignments put students out in the field. One form of this is exposing students to other cultures through international travel doing OD work or in presenting at an international conference. Participant (F1) desires to expose and "immerse" students into other "cultural contexts and trying to do OD work." Faculty member (F18) agreed,

> so many [doctoral] programs don't have travel.... It transforms the student who doesn't have knowledge of being in another part of the world.... I don't know of too many programs that make travel and international OD explicit.

Faculty member (F1) described the reflective work that students carry out in debriefing their experiences from an international practicum:

> I take students out there to a different country and they do their practicum. I think that this part helps with their skills of self-reflection. They understand themselves, and they understand their culture better when they come back, because I think in working in a different cultural setting, it stretches their comfort zone and it is very difficult. So when they come back, only then do they realize that they have a different lens to look at their own culture and themselves. So that is what adds to their development, I think.... We cannot understand the idea of social justice until we are pushed out and are a minority in a different culture—where we feel like aliens. It is actually a shift in the mind.

This professor intentionally used the international practicum experience to help students discover more about themselves and their own culture through self-reflection. In addition, this professor hopes that it broadens the students' perspective to understand better the minority position through the cross-cultural experience. Faculty member (F6) described the practicum experiences of students. This program has

> a practicum every year. I think that is unique about us. I don't think anyone else requires three practicum. And I see practica as where things get tested out. People start to integrate theory with the skills—how to do it. The practica and the debriefing from the practica..... The first year the practica could be a variety of things: it can be shadowing, it can be interviewing, simple interventions, depending on people's background. Second year is intervention in a team. Third year is independently.

According to faculty member (F6), the skill base of the student is tested, and the integration of theory and practice begins to happen in the practicum experiences and the debriefing of these experiences.

A couple of faculty members mentioned another way they assess the development of their students. These professors compare the incoming résumé of the student with the postdissertation curriculum vitae or résumé. Faculty member (F18) stated,

> At application time, they have submitted a résumé … a one pager with the two or three organizations they have worked for. Look at what has happened over three years, where there is a whole other page or two about presentations and publications and consulting opportunities. I think that is a measurement of how we can look at how well the people have developed.

Faculty member (F11) spoke of another type of stop-check progress assignment: "At the end of the first year and the second year we are asking them to list their professional affiliations and their articles and so forth. That keeps them focused on what's the name of the game." This professor urges students to stay aware of their own development and progress by regularly making a list of the intentional contributions and opportunities they have taken advantage of since starting the doctoral program.

Dissertation

Several faculty members spoke about using the dissertation as a means of evaluation of student's development. Participant (F4) stated,

> The final assessment as to whether students have been successful in learning is the completion of a rigorous dissertation to the standards of the committee. The committee always has one of our faculty members and two other committee members from other leading universities in the fields of OB, OD, leadership, et cetera. The dissertations have to meet the standards of those external reviewers as well.

The above quote speaks to the rigor and standards for assessment of the dissertations in this program. Faculty member (F12) agreed and adds,

> I think assessing learning outcomes really comes out in the dissertation process. In fact, we have had several examples of people using systematic methods to assess what is going on in their firms and as a result, not only contribute to practice but also to theory. The whole idea is you see what the issue is and collect historical data or find some way of approaching what is going on here in a systematic way so that you not only advance theory as a by-product but also solve the issue which is going on in the firm using more systematic methods versus using a fly-by-night approach, so to speak.

This professor noted the bridging of the theory-practice gap as students are encouraged to conduct research studies in their own organizations and use this work for their dissertation projects. The notion of research that actually improves the organization is also in view in the above quote. Faculty member (F8) promoted another view of the dissertation process:

> I have a constant difference with a very practical senior faculty colleague who believes that "A good dissertation is a done dissertation." And I am the one who counterpoints saying, "No, a good dissertation is one that you may not want to quit but you have to." In other words, passion-driven and meaningful and contributory is my language.... Both of these ways of doing a dissertation are meant to take you to the next level, which is "What you are going to do with it?" But it has become more clear to me that you have got to care about what you are doing at a pretty high level to keep you getting up early in the morning or staying up late at night and with no supervision except your own supervision, essentially. I think that the remarkable nature of a doctoral program is that you know that after this, you are responsible for your learning, and if we could figure out how to do that in the first grade, we would have a little different world.

This professor wants students to have passion around their dissertation topics, igniting an intrinsic motivation to learn. As a by-product, students increasingly understand that they are responsible for their own meaningful learning. The idea is that working through the dissertation process not only helps a person grow as a researcher but it may also stretch the individual in other more personal ways. Faculty member (F6) alluded to this personal growth in saying, "I think a lot of learning in dissertations goes beyond the subject ... learning about loneliness, hanging in there, all sorts of things." Additionally, professor (F6) stated that the implication of this is that the mentoring of the student in the dissertation process can be about more than completing the research project.

Two categories of findings have been explored thus far: the learning outcomes and creating a learning environment. The last category of findings, based on faculty interviews, explores the indicators of successful graduates. The following section will delve into this topic.

INDICATORS OF SUCCESSFUL ALUMNI

The last section of findings from the interviews with faculty fall under one category; this overarching category is an indicator of successful alumni. This section looks at the third research question: "What do doctoral faculty identify as indicators of successful graduates of their programs, and what is the nature of these indicators of success?" Six themes surface in respect to indicators of successful alumni. The six themes are (a) postgraduate publications, (b) contributing to the profession, (c) a strong professional performance, (d) an ability to critically reflect, (e) a learning posture, and (f) helping others to learn.

Postgraduate Publications

According to faculty interviews, the first theme that emerged with regard to indicators of successful graduates is postgraduate publications. Faculty member (F4) argued this point in saying an indicator of successful graduates

> is productivity in terms of continuing to publish and contribute to the field, because a big part of what helps to advance the field is the writing and the creation of tools and processes and activities and so on. If you see productivity in those areas, I think that that is a sign of a successful graduate.

Participant (F5) simply stated, as graduates of a "practitioner-scholar program,"

> I want them to write. I want them to add to the field of knowledge, but they are not going to be publishing in Academy of Management Journals. They are going to be in *Practitioner,* they are going to be in *Training and Development,* and they are going to be in management journals.

Another faculty member, (F13), maintained,

> Certainly I look at those of our graduates who produce good research, and that makes me proud. If that research is published—the better the places it is published in, the more proud, just because I know how difficult those are. But I don't think research is only judged by where it is published because there is a lot of research that is innovative that is hard to get into the higher-prestige journals. So I also look at the research in terms of the creativity. Are they tackling a social issue, a need, a phenomenon that nobody else has looked at or tackled in that way—seems important to me.

It is interesting that both of the previous two quotes from professors spoke about what types of publication they desire for their alumni to work toward. Yet the types of publications are at different ends of the scholar-practitioner continuum. Faculty member (F18) provided a disclaimer:

> I don't think that amount of publishing is *the* indicator of successful scholar-practitioners. I think it's *an* indicator. It's *an* indicator because you could spend the rest of your life sitting at a desk publishing and it is not going to enhance the practitioner side. It's that and more.

Graduates are expected to add to the knowledge base, but as scholar-practitioners, there is also an expectation to impact practice.

Contributing Professionals

In addition to producing postgraduate publications, field contributions were also mentioned by faculty as an indicator of successful graduates. Faculty member (F11) succinctly stated that successful alumni are "contributing professionals in the field and have a true appreciation for what it means to be a professional in the field." Participant (F5) believes that successful alumni are "excellent consultants" in the broad sense of the term "consultant." More specifically, faculty member (F6) stated that successful alumni are "able to diagnosis and help people figure out whatever intervention may be valuable, that is, using the traditional OD skillset." Faculty member (F12) went beyond the mastery of OD practitioner skills and stated that the successful doctoral graduate is a "practitioner-scholar … someone who actually has one foot in the world of practice and one foot in the world of theory, so someone who is able to sort of effortlessly go back and forth." In addition, participant (F12) has the concern that graduates

> have done impactful work in their companies, but the difficulty is that they have not taken the time to write about these experiences. Because again, the whole idea is to not only impact practice but also to impact theory in the process of doing so. That is where I think that people are lacking, and that has been my sense.

Faculty member (F13) mentioned another type of desired contribution of successful alumni: to start new academic programs and promote program innovation with existing graduate programs. Participant (F13) stated, "I am very proud of many of our doctoral graduates who have had a profound impact on institutions by creating new master's programs, et cetera." Thus, contributions through practice in both the corporate and academic worlds were mentioned by faculty in the interviews.

Strong Professional Performance

A third indicator of success mentioned by the faculty is strong professional performance on the part of the alumni. Faculty member (F9) observed that successful doctoral graduates "will be able to have an amazing impact in their organizations or the organizations that they choose to work with." Increasing the strength of professional performance of the graduate is held in high regard by participant (F2):

I think one indicator is success in their work; whether they choose to go academically or they choose to go into an organization. I think we see it in how well they perform, how well they move up in their organizations. If they go the academic route, you look for the next round of presentations, the next round of writing, not the first and the second, but it is kind of the next round when people start to get into the stride and they start to integrate stuff.... They become more credible. They become more influential. They are easier to listen to—they make better arguments. They often do straddle that theory and practice well. And of course, I give extra points for that because a lot of academics don't do that very well.

The sense of ongoing continued professional growth was communicated in the above statement; regardless of context, whether in an academic environment or a corporation, strong growth in performance was what was in view. Faculty member (F14) added that successful alumni have "the ability to take on bigger challenges in their current organizations and/or to make a successful shift to a new organization." Professor (F14) went on to say that when a graduate makes this successful transition to a new organization,

in some instances they may not take on a bigger challenge but because of what they have learned about themselves they figure out that they need to be in a different organization, and they may make that move launching themselves onto a new trajectory that may lead them to a higher level of responsibility in a new organization.

Bigger challenges and new challenges based on new more authentic self-knowledge was what this faculty member deemed successful. Another professor, (F1), made a similar observation:

Many of our graduates change their jobs. They were able to find jobs that they like. Because they went through personal transformation, they somehow shifted and became more aware of what makes them happy in their jobs and say, "This is the job I have always dreamed about." They look for jobs that meet their needs and utilize their talents and new skills and maybe even they have found "a new me" and they try to meet the interests of this new person in them.

This professor believes that successful alumni have the courage and confidence to seek out and step into a new professional position that resonates with the "personal transformation" that happened in doctoral studies and, as a result, utilizes their unique talents more effectively. Faculty member (F6) stated that successful graduates are "people who get new jobs that they wouldn't have gotten without the educational experience; people who move up or into more creative work." Faculty member (F5) gave a summary list of indicators of successful graduates: "We are looking at promotions, new jobs, more responsibilities, going to a consulting firm, being an adjunct or faculty member at some university, and publications."

Postgraduate publications, contributing to the field through effective OD practice, and growing stronger in professional performance are indicators of successful alumni that faculty have mentioned in interviews.

Ability to Critically Reflect

Successful alumni have the ability to critically reflect according to several faculty members. Professor (F1) remarked that the successful graduate is

> a reflective practitioner; they want to think critically; the one who actually does change in reality and not just talk about it, not just say the right words and behave differently; and people see that and then they see that there is a gap between espoused values and the values by which you actually live; that they will not fear the change, and they will actually promote social justice and do some meaningful work.

Participant (F1) highlighted the ability to critically reflect in such a way that it actually affects one's visible behavior, and there is congruence in espoused values and values used in practice. Professor (F16) observed that successful alumni

> have incorporated this habit of critical reflection into their own practice so that as they negotiated their own lives as practitioners, they would be much more alert to the assumptions that they were making about different situations that they came across and different problems that they were working through, and they would be willing to study those assumptions and decide when they were accurate and when they needed reframing—so that I think that that critically reflective habit would be second nature, and I would also hope that graduates would be sufficiently aware of that habit to mentor colleagues in becoming critically reflective and to know enough about the dynamics of how you learn to challenge assumptions to be able to bring colleagues to looking at assumptions critically in ways that didn't come across as threatening or intimidating. So those would be the sorts of things that I would be looking for in graduates—that exercise of critical reflection as a kind of daily habit.

> Interviewer: For OD consultants, you mentioned that an indicator of a successful graduate would be to be able to mentor people in knowing how to critically reflect. Do you believe that OD consultants can do that with organizations?

F16:　Oh yeah. I think that that is probably—I don't know that I would say that it is *the* most valuable function, but it is certainly one the most valuable functions that the consultant can do, because you are usually hired to improve some kind of process or to erase or reduce some kind of problem or difficulty. I think that understanding the assumptions that frame how people define this problem or understand the assumptions behind a strategic initiative and judging whether those assumptions are correct and the way that other people experience those assumptions. I mean, that is very much a part of what consultants and developers do. They help people just get better at knowing what assumptions claim organizational life and individual practices, and checking those. I have done work with lots of different organizations—military, private, corporate— and I would say that the thing that ties together a lot of what I do is helping people become aware of assumptions that are kind of taken for granted, and they are part of the woodwork, and they're enshrined in the mission statement, and they frame the way they typically set up teams and the way that problems are approached. And being critically reflective is just saying, "Hang on. Before we move forward with this, let's just make sure we know the assumptions that we are taking seriously and decide whether they are accurate."

The above exchange highlighted that successful alumni habitually practice critical reflection, mentor others in the process of learning to critically reflect, and guide organizations in corporately understanding assumptions that inform organizational life and practice. Alongside of the ability to critically reflect, a learning posture was identified as a theme that emerged as an indicator of successful graduates.

A Learning Posture

Faculty members mentioned a love of learning as an indicator of successful alumni. Professor (F4) believes a successful doctoral graduate "revels in the joy of discovery, of exploring the world, of exploring ideas and their application in the real world with just a total love and vigor." Faculty member (F18) agrees and added,

I think an indicator of success is when the veneer is off and they recognize that they don't know everything. I think that an indicator of success in OD is this element of humility…. I think that an indicator of success is that person who wants and enjoys being a lifetime learner and has a level of humility to know that they will never know it all.

A love of learning seems to go hand-in-hand with a posture of humility, especially with regard to what one does not know. Professor (F18) told a story of an alumnus who typifies this idea of humility,

> A lifelong learner ... "Butterflies in the belly." We heard it from an alumnus who said, "I was in Training and Development, and I knew everything, and I had it down pat. I knew it by rote. But then I went into OD with that same expectation. And because I didn't know it, it gave me butterflies in my belly. Here I am with a doctorate in OD, and I still get butterflies." Because you *don't know* it; it is the ambiguity and the unknown. If you are a person who can't deal with that uncertainty, you probably wouldn't be a good person for OD.

The above example underscored that being a lifelong learner means being self-aware that one does not know it all and does not pretend to know it all, but continues to seek after knowledge, even in the midst of an uncertain situation where there are nervous "butterflies in the belly." Professor (F18) stated that "the dissertation and the three years in the program are just the springboard.... There is something transformative along the way," which leads the successful graduate toward becoming a lifelong learner.

Helping Others to Learn

Helping others to learn was also mentioned as an indicator of successful alumni. People who love to learn naturally want to share what they learn with others. Faculty member (F10) pointed this out in saying,

> I think probably the most applicable measure of success would be whether or not they seek to share what they learn with others. Because if they don't seek to share that knowledge and communicate that experience, whether they are in a four-person team or a four-thousand person organization, it doesn't matter what industry they work in or anything else, what profession. If they are willing to reach out to others and share that knowledge and experience, they are successful.

A willingness to share what is learned but also the skill to know how to help people learn is necessary. Professor (F15) stated, "I want them to be good educators—people who can design and carry out effective learning environments whether that is in the classroom or in an organization." An additional element in helping others to learn is being a knowledge creator. Faculty member (F4) believes that a successful graduate "is someone who really cares about developing great knowledge and skill at a very high level of excellence so that they can contribute to the greatest degree possible."

Developing knowledge that helps make an impactful contribution is significant. Having a learning posture and wanting to help others learn focuses attention outward. Faculty member (F4) maintained that a successful graduate is someone

> who is really committed to building a better world by helping people develop, by helping organizations get better, by helping society thrive, and whether it's a big way or small way, depending on what type of job they have or role they play, that that is something that they want to do—a legacy they want to leave with their life…. I think that indicators of successful graduates are if after graduating from the program, they go out into the world and make a positive difference. And I know that that is a very subjective kind of thing, but you know it when you see it. These people are really investing in other people and organizations to build a better world.

Six themes of indicators of successful alumni surfaced from the findings. The six themes are (a) postgraduate publications, (b) contributing to the profession, (c) a strong professional performance, (d) an ability to critically reflect, (e) a learning posture, and (f) helping others to learn. The views of the alumni are the focus of the next chapter.

NOTE

1. These seven learning outcomes are not ranked according to any particular order of importance.

CHAPTER 6

ALUMNI PERSPECTIVES

The previous chapter looked at the research findings from the interviews with doctoral faculty. This chapter explores the research findings from interviews with doctoral graduates regarding their educational experience and the impact that they believe it had on them. The three sections of findings are reported in this chapter are (a) important learning, (b) factors influencing learning and development, and (c) self-reported contributions to the field.

IMPORTANT LEARNING

The first section looks at the important learning that occurred during doctoral education from the perspectives of alumni as reported in their interviews. The research question that guided this section of findings was, "What do doctoral alumni identify as the most important learning that occurred while in their doctoral program?" Four themes emerged from the alumni interviews. The four themes of important learning are that doctoral education (a) provided intellectual challenge, (b) instilled discipline and commitment, (c) fostered confidence and humility, and (d) promoted life change. Each of these themes will be explored below.

Provided Intellectual Challenge

Several doctoral alumni spoke about the intellectual challenge that their doctorate studies provided them. Two aspects of intellectual challenge surfaced in the interviews. The first theme reported by alumni was that shifts in their thinking about important issues took place, and secondly, a broadening of their perspectives happened as a result of their doctoral education.

A Shift in Thinking

Several alumni spoke about how their thinking had shifted as a result of their doctoral education. For example, participant (A18) described a shift in thinking regarding theories of change: "When we were doing the AI work, that was very exciting rethinking the approach to OD, so that it is not so problem focused—much more positive—it sounds simple, but it really changed a lot of my thinking around that." The previous quote highlighted a shift in thinking about practice that happened for a student during a practicum experience. Other shifts in thinking happened during classroom dialogue. The interaction below with participant (A19) provides an example of a dramatic paradigm shift that took place for this alumnus:

> A19: The expectation that I had at the beginning, and I was reflecting on that near the end of my program, was I was looking for the perfect management solutions to the things I was facing at work…. The reality is my whole framework around how I thought about management and leadership and governance and so on changed during the course of that program; so I was looking for something at the beginning, and I ended up in a completely different place at the end.
>
> Interviewer: Can you summarize some of those learnings that had shifted?
>
> A19: Well, I think that—and my professor played a pretty important role—it's the whole framework or paradigm that I had around searching for—there must be a solution to this issue some place—the one right answer. And what he did, and other faculty members did, was force all of us as students to look at that paradigm and say, "Perhaps that is not the paradigm that will be helpful going into the future." And there was a real thinking shift, and that took place over a period of time, and so it was really an eye-opening experience. So for me, it was very much a philosophical shift; and at the same time then, along with the philosophical shift, there was a lot of new content and new ideas, and so it was very interesting…. I believe that the whole way that I look at things has changed. At my very core things have changed. Maybe that sounds kind of nebulous. I have

> moved from a scenario where I approached every problem as a problem to be solved—a problem that there is a solution to—to a recognition that there are some problems that can't be solved; they are paradoxes; they are polarities. Then the question is from a leadership management perspective or an OD perspective, especially for those very difficult polarities; what do you do to manage those and make sure that the people that you are working with and that you are leading are not looking at these as problems to be solved but looking at them as things that have to be managed? There are things in the world of OD and leadership where you encounter those complex issues that by their very nature are complex. How do you resolve those? How do you manage those? So the way that I approach that today—one of the faculty members used to say, "It just depends." And so that is much more of a pragmatic way of approaching things. So my style has changed I think.

The lengthy interaction points out a number of things. A shift in thinking occurred for this alumnus that was expansive and deep; it occurred over time, and it was brought on by the influence of the faculty in asking challenging questions and providing thought-provoking content. The graduate's idea of leadership moved from being responsible for finding solutions to problems, to helping people realize that not everything is a problem to be solved, but rather some things are polarities to be managed. This person also seems to have become more comfortable with the idea of ambiguity and complexity in practice. The last thing that alumnus (A19) hinted at was that this shift in thinking led to a change in behavior, a change in the practice of leadership; at a minimum, this person was wondering how to lead with these new discoveries in mind. Participant (A30) also made observations about changes experienced as a result of the degree. Doctoral education,

> imposed much more discipline in my thinking and my behavior, business behavior. There were no more off-the-cuff things, or if it is off-the-cuff, I seek to understand why. So it made me, I think, much more prudent, but not in a scarce sort of way or an indecisive sort of way, but a much more prudent conservative businessman, in a good sense of the word. Well-thought through. It helped me in that.

This alumnus appeared to become more deliberate and reasoned in decision making, thinking through business issues, and in "business behavior" as a result of the doctoral education. Participant (A35) added to this idea:

> There is nothing that I am going to do professionally that is more challenging than writing a dissertation ... the quality of my thinking and my intellect when up significant levels—I feel with great confidence that there is nothing you are going to give me that I can't read and understand and make sense of.

This person attributed increases in "quality of thinking," competency, and confidence due to the experience of doctoral education.

Developing or deepening the ability to think critically was also mentioned by doctoral graduates. Participant (A7) maintained that as a result of doctoral education, "I changed in critical thinking. I look at things differently. I often look at things as an opportunity to do research or how can I solve a problem." In addition to growth in critical thinking, the previous quote highlighted a shift in orientation toward looking outward through a problem-solving research lens. Alumnus (A14) maintained,

> For me, doctoral education was a monumental stretch. How did it stretch me? Cognitive skills, you know, learning new subjects. Learning from my classmates was a huge part of the learning experience. For one thing, there were people from all over the world, so I learned about areas of the world that I didn't know much about.

Participant (A14) named the intellectual growth that occurred as being stretched in "cognitive skills," and part of that growth and learning was attributed to the interactions with the diverse members of the cohort. Alumnus (A25) maintained that the doctoral program "teaches you to read effectively. It teaches you to distill data. It teaches you to write. It teaches you to learn."

Alumni mentioned several ways in which their thinking was challenged or stretched. Shifts occurred in both what they thought about certain topics (e.g., theories of change, philosophy of leadership) and in their quality of thought life (e.g., more disciplined and deliberate thinking, increased critical thinking, and the more frequent use of a researcher lens to view the world).

A Broader Perspective

Alumni also made reference to having their perspectives broadened through the experience of doctoral education. Participant (A33) simply stated,

> I think I am a lot more open-minded about some things, look at things from a different perspective. Okay, I see things from a thirty-thousand-foot level versus on the ground level. I think I'm a little bit more détached in some ways, when I analyze situations.

Likewise, respondent (A32) stated that doctoral education experience,

makes me think in ways that I have never thought before. My windows are wider, my doors are open larger—you see things from a perspective that is not such a narrow tunnel. You take quite the high view. You say "Yeah that may be true, but I bet that there are other ways to look at this." I find myself constantly questioning things that I probably wouldn't have been questioning before.

Both (A33) and (A32) spoke about seeing issues from an aerial vantage point and being more open, inquisitive, and analytical. Another example comes from alumnus (A17):

Doctoral education certainly made me more aware of the world we live in. Typically, most folks at the bachelor's or master's level that have full-time employment in a technical area, like I do, they are working the project and designing the next rocket motor or the next bridge. For most of those folks, it is head down and pencils wagging on the yellow pad. They are focused on whatever project they are assigned, and they are worried about that project plan. They are worried about their piece of that plan and executing to schedule and under cost. They are worried about those kinds of things, and that is what they pay attention to, and the fact that what they are doing has a global impact, or potentially has a global impact, generally doesn't cross their mind. Having gone through this program and gotten this degree, I don't worry as much about the pencil and the yellow pad as I worry about the global impacts of what is being done. It causes me to look more globally, to be more globally aware, and not just from the standpoint of what will this do to people in France, Saudi Arabia, and South Africa. It is not so much that as it is what I do today is going to impact people to the left, to the right of me, forward, backward, above, and below. It increases that awareness that it is not just about me as an individual; there are impacts and effects out beyond just my little sphere.

This doctoral graduate observed the shift in thinking that took place from an individualistic and technical orientation to a much broader awareness of the effects of one's actions locally and globally. Alumnus (A31) described a similar realization:

I think I am less excited about solving business-performance problems of profitability or reducing costs, which used to excite me.... I recognize the importance, and so I don't think that I trivialize the business problems. I still like business problems, but I am less interested in those and more interested in ideas, personal vision, and growth in leadership, because I think those could have the second-order impact on others and on the business as a consequent. I feel it has made me place a greater emphasis on human beings and human capital, and it fits well with my own philosophy of where I think I can make the most contributions.

Participant (A31) described a different type of shift in thinking that occurred during doctoral studies as an "epiphany." Respondent (A31) states,

> In the very first residency in the doctoral program, prior students came and talked about how it is extremely important to narrow your scope, to be very laser focused on an area where you think you might make a contribution, but even then after you think about that, narrow it even further and just really concentrate on something reasonably simplified and narrow, otherwise you are never going to be able to—in the time frame that we had in mind—be able to do the study, do the research, write the dissertation, and graduate. I nearly quit at the end of that residency. That is not why I came to the doctoral program. I really wanted to do something that was complex and difficult and challenging. This whole idea of simplifying didn't appeal to me. And that night I had an epiphany that changed my thinking; and the epiphany was the inversion of product and process. And I will explain that to you. My ingoing assumption was that the product is the dissertation of this doctoral study and the three years is the process. And it struck me that night that I had gotten it backwards and that the process of going through three or four years is the product that I am really buying and the dissertation is the proof of the process. And so what I was really buying into was immersing myself into a process, and that is what the doctorate offered. In that process, I was going to be exposed to new ideas, new tools, new techniques, new discussions, and it was going to enliven my zest for new ideas in a way that I could not have continuing to pursue my life as a consultant or an executive. And that just got me reignited about it all.

This participant was able to shift from focusing solely on the dissertation as "the product" of education to understanding that the immersion in study and the personal and professional learning from that immersion were the greatest benefit. The role of the dissertation in this person's educational paradigm moved from "the product" of education to "the proof of the process." This represents a shift in thinking about the nature and purpose of education.

In this segment, alumni spoke about becoming more open-minded, being detached and analytical, taking an aerial vantage point, being more globally aware, and placing a greater emphasis on human capital. A broader perspective and a shift in thinking were two themes related to intellectual challenge as reported by alumni.

Instilled Discipline and Commitment

Instilling discipline and commitment was another element of important learning that doctoral alumni mentioned in their interviews. Several alumni commented on the discipline and commitment it took to complete a doctoral degree. Participant (A25) simply stated, "The doctoral program is very demanding, so it teaches you the discipline of managing your time and managing your priorities." Growth in the ability to manage time wisely was also noted by alumnus (A11): "I think personally, it took me to another level of developing those time-management skills. Not that I was bad all along. But if you are used to juggling two things and now you have three or four, that is very different." In addition to time-management skills, another element of self-discipline mentioned by alumnus (A10) was the awareness of living out one's priorities and the tension that brings to the surface during doctoral studies:

> I think it stretches you as a person because it challenges you; I mean, it is not something you can separate from your life. When you decide to do this, you live it. You live it not only when you show up at class, but you live it from what you take home, and your family lives it, and your friends live with it … I am a high-off-the-charts "E" in Myers Brigg—an insane "E"—and so I had to tuck in all my edges, and I didn't see my friends as much and my spouse had to be very understanding … from a personal standpoint, it is both challenging and requires that you become much more aware about what is important.

The sacrifice for this extroverted person of giving up time with family and friends to focus on doctoral work was taxing; there was an acute awareness of the effect that this had on the people in this graduate's life. Alumnus (A4) believes that

> There is a lot of pressure to make these programs easier on people so that they can get through it; however … what I learned here and why I changed was because it was so difficult to get through. And I think that the pressure to make it easier—I don't think that you should make it too easy. When you make it too easy, you give up the change, the struggle. There is value in the struggle.

Participant (A4) was concerned that there may be pressure to ease up on doctoral candidates so as to make it less difficult for them to complete the degree. However, the belief of this alumnus is that the challenge of the rigor helps develop the person.

A different example of self-discipline was given by alumnus (A5)

Doctoral education is about being self-taught. My skillset that I was there to develop is how to teach myself to learn. And I did that. And the students that expect it to be spoon-fed to them are going to be sorely disappointed.

This alumnus talked about being a self-directed learner and realizing the discipline to do that was a big part of doctoral education. In a similar way, participant (A10) stated,

I don't think I will remember the courses that I took. I don't think I will remember much of the content. I will remember what it took to get through it, and the rigor, and the way that my *being* changed as a result of it.

It is interesting that this person attributes the avenue of being shaped or changed in "being" was as a result of the rigorous process of doctoral education rather than the other factors that were named. In speaking about the "rigorous process of research" alumnus (A10) argued,

You get some fundamental knowledge that grounds you in how to do that, so that's what I took away. But the experience at the same time has built a different set of muscles, and it is three years of lifting, three years of training.... And so you are not going to go through that without some kind of change; and so for lack of a better word, there is some sort of personal strength that emerged I can't necessarily put my finger on. But I see it in most of my colleagues ... you can see the strength built in people. And that is exciting.

The analogy between weight lifting and the rigors of research illustrate both the hard work and determination to reach a goal. Over several years of practice, new strength was gained, and people were transformed, according to participant (A10). Alumnus (A13) also spoke about the strong effects of the rigorous dissertation process:

I was trying to explain to my spouse why I was so emotional about finishing my dissertation, and my spouse said, "It sounds like you put everything into it; everything emotionally, spiritually, intellectually, and physically into this, and you are afraid that it still might not be enough." So it was that fear of not just failing, but of just devastating loss of putting so much into something and it not being enough. That was something totally foreign to me, and that was my biggest personal growth. I remember somebody saying afterward, "You must be really proud of your accomplishment." And this was sort of when I was still suffering from postdissertation stress disorder, and I said, "Not pride. No. Pride is not the emotion—grateful—relieved. All of those things, but not pride." Because I cut it so close—it was too hard to take pride in the accomplishment ... it was just too hard. To this day I don't feel pride. I still feel grateful—they call it a terminal degree for a reason.

This quote magnifies overcoming the fear of failure, being perseverant, committed to finishing the goal, and the tremendous amount of effort it took for this alumnus to complete the doctoral degree.

The doctoral degree instilled discipline and commitment in several ways, according to alumni. Graduates report increased growth in time-management skills, managing priorities, being a self-directed learner, increased strength, overcoming fear of failure, and perseverance through the rigorous dissertation process.

Fostered Confidence and Humility

In addition to providing intellectual challenge and instilling discipline and commitment, fostering confidence and humility was a third theme that alumni named as important learning in their doctoral education. This section explores this theme from three perspectives. Some doctoral graduates reported growing in confidence, others reported growing in humility, and still others reported growing in both confidence and humility.

Growth in Confidence

Alumnus (A20) stated that doctoral education

> helped me to identify some things about my interests, and my goals, and my values … and it shaped me as a person. It also did give me confidence … I started to think, "I actually can succeed in this program. I do have what it takes to be at this level." So I gained self-confidence.

Graduate (A20) spoke about a general sense of added confidence. Similarly, alumnus (A7) simply stated,

> I am more confident with who I am, what I contribute. I engage in forums at conferences on subject matters that are very important to me, which prior to the doctorate program, I probably wouldn't have because I didn't feel like I could contribute anything, or I didn't have any credibility in that field. So it allowed that access; it allowed that credibility that I needed.

As a result of increased confidence, this person now feels empowered to join in collegial conversations with other professionals. Likewise, participant (A10) maintained, "I think that it has made me realize that I can speak with much more confidence and … a more declarative fashion without making excuses for what I believe to be true." The previous two quotes from (A7) and (A10) point to the increased confidence these graduates have in their ability to persuasively articulate their own thoughts.

Another form of expression of confidence was stated by alumni. Several alumni spoke of their increased confidence in their practitioner contributions. For example, participant (A15) maintained, as the result of doctoral education,

> I know I have definitely changed in many different ways. It has been kind of a path of discovery. I am trying to reflect back on when I started the program and where I was at. I would say I have more confidence in the work that I do and what I can provide. Within a lot of organizations, there are ups and downs; nobody's job is secure in today's economic times. If anything happened, I have a lot of confidence I would get a job pretty much anywhere else. I don't think I maybe would have had that before in the past.

This person spoke of confidence in practitioner abilities that was not as strong prior to the educational experience. Participant (A25) linked the doctoral education to being in a "better place" professionally. Alumnus (A25) stated,

> After I got my doctorate, I didn't want to do the job I was currently doing. I thought that I could do much better than I was doing. And so I made it a point of looking for opportunities where I could make a difference. It gave me a lot more confidence.... I think that it has made me a stronger, more confident person in what I do. I think that professionally, I am in a better place than I was before I was in the program. It has benefitted me economically, financially, professionally—in many ways.

This graduate sought out and attained a more challenging professional position, in part due to confidence gained from completing doctoral work. Participant (A35) spoke about the confidence that was gained from doctoral education and as a result, stepping into new opportunities. Respondent (A35) stated,

> I thought it was "get a degree and become a doctor." I didn't realize all of the opportunities it creates. It opens doors. I have been given opportunities with this degree to do things that I could have never done without the degree.... I can't believe the deep water that I am swimming in. I could never have done it without the degree, without the OD knowledge, and without staying *true* to research. It is phenomenal how it has changed me because it has given me the confidence .... I couldn't be going on the tenure track without this degree.... It has given me the opportunity and the confidence that I so much needed.

In the larger corpus of the transcription, participant (A35) describes some of the many different avenues of opportunities that came about as a result of doctoral education. Alumnus (A18) maintained, as a result of doctoral education,

> I have developed more confidence. I have developed my own theories of practice.... I have been doing a lot of publishing. I am writing a book. I don't think I would have been able to do that without a doctorate.

The quotations from this brief section point to confidence gained through doctoral work that affected people who work as practitioners, consultants, and academics.

Growth in Humility

Several alumni mentioned growing in confidence as a result of participating in doctoral studies. This section looks at a different response to the doctoral education process. Growth in humility is the focus of this brief section. For example, participant (A27) revealed,

> One of the things that the doctorate showed me is how much I don't know. I am so aware of how much information there is on any given subject and how many different interventions there are and things people do to reengineer large organizations and those folks leading at what they know—it's just mind boggling to me. It has actually humbled me because I understand that there is so much out there that I don't know.

This person was humbled when confronted with the vast amounts of knowledge available, realizing that it is more than anyone could possibly know. Alumnus (A36) noted a shift that has taken place:

> I came into the doctoral program knowing everything, and I left knowing nothing. I came into the doctoral program willing to reach quick conclusions about complex topics based on the opinions that I brought to the topic.... I read an article once that had the term "metacognition," which is the science of studying different points of view, and I left doctoral education with the ability to study another point of view without having to necessarily embrace or react to it.

This person came to the realization that other perspectives were worth considering, and this forces one to hold one's own opinion in suspension while another point of view is examined. Respondent (A1) described a shift that took place:

> A1:   One of the things that prior to pursuing my doctorate degree I realize from my 360s is I have great confidence.... [During doctoral education] I was able to kind of be more humble in that confidence because I have seen what I did not see before.

> While my confidence before created a barrier between me and others, my confidence after three years of education became a little bit more humble. I became more aware of what I didn't know.

Interviewer: What do you attribute that to?

A1:   If I want to speculate, I would say that at the doctorate level, you interact with top minds of the country; whereas, probably in my work environment, I interact with my peers ... within my comfort zone, within my circle of influence, I felt very confident. But now it made me aware of my own shortcomings because I always compared myself to my surroundings ... I was able to see the strengths of others that I did not encounter outside of the degree.

The growth in humility that this person experienced was in tempering the confidence that already existed.

Growth in Confidence and Humility

Several alumni mention the juxtaposition of growth in both confidence and humility as a result of their doctoral education. Two quotes below illustrate this theme. Participant (A26) believes that

> When you know more, you are more comfortable on understanding issues, and it gives you self-confidence. I think that if you understand the evolution of science and understanding how science works and how theories are built, it also helps you in some respect be more critical of it. The change is your increase in confidence, but perhaps you are more aware of how little you know about certain topics. Perhaps by knowing more, you become more humble about the things you say, because by going deep in certain areas, it makes you more humble, because you really know how much you don't know ... even about your own topic. It also gives you more confidence, on the other hand, to handle some things. You get some confidence by knowing more, but in other areas, you get humbled and respect other people and perhaps know more of your place to hear and to listen to other people.

Respondent (A26) fully stepped into the paradox of confidence and humility; knowing more makes you realize how much you do not know. This person also seemed to be working with the tension of knowing when to speak and when to listen. Participant (A35) also reflected on the confidence-humility tension:

> There is nothing that I am going to do professionally that is more challenging than [writing a dissertation] ... the quality of my thinking and my intellect went up significant levels—I feel with great confidence that there is nothing you are going to give me that I can't read and understand and make sense of.... I am confident in my reading. I am also confident in my

writing and on an even greater level. I can write well, and I own that now. I would not have said that earlier. I can write well enough to convey ideas, so I am very confident about that. I have always been a decent presenter, but I am a much better presenter now. I think the confidence of the doctorate behind me kicked me up a level. Professionally, I have got a major boost in self-confidence across the board.... Yet I am more humble, to be honest with you. That might sound a little counterintuitive because I recognize how people can make a big deal about of the doctorate degree; but I see it for what it is. I was privileged to be able to have this experience. I was privileged to have the resources; but I am not on a pedestal at all. So it has humbled me.... The other thing it has done is that it has helped me to put things in perspective ... I know people with a doctorate, and I know people without a doctorate, and it doesn't make you the smartest person on the planet, and it doesn't make you special—you were positioned to be able to do something and you took advantage of it. I think even more than getting a doctorate, it really allowed me to really see how privileged I was.

The boost in self-confidence is made abundantly clear in the above statement: confidence gained in many different arenas. Alongside of growth in confidence came a stark realization that the privilege of doctoral education is not afforded to everyone, and that realization had a humbling effect on this person. The personal growth that happened within these doctoral alumni is evident. Some grew in confidence, others in humility, and yet others in both confidence and humility.

Thus far, three of the four overarching themes of important learning have been discussed. According to alumni, doctoral education has (a) provided intellectual challenge, (b) instilled discipline and commitment, and (c) fostered confidence and humility. The last section will focus on how doctoral education promoted life change.

Promoted Life Change

A final category of important learning was identified from the interviews with alumni. Several graduates report that their doctoral education experience promoted life change. For example, alumnus (A4) stated that the educational experience

turned out to be a lot more than I thought. I went into the program thinking that this will be great. I will have more options; I will learn some things, but I didn't think that it would change *me*.... I didn't think it would change fundamentally who I am, and it did.

The previous quote highlights the unexpectedness of the change this person experienced; whereas alumnus (A2) was given fair warning regarding the change that can occur within doctoral students during their educational process,

> I remember one of our faculty members said early on that the life experience of achieving a doctorate will change you as an individual, and I think that is very true. I believe that I am a different individual once I left the program.... and I don't think that it is the four-year differential; I think it is the process one goes through to achieve that type of degree.

Alumnus (A28) stated regarding doctoral education,

> Personal growth was the biggest thing for me. Just realizing that learning and development is not so scary, and it is really a great thing and something that you want to have ... to embrace it more, and to find myself, and to find a direction, and that has been very helpful.

All three of these introductory quotes point to the inner change that happened within these individuals as a result of completing a doctoral degree. To unpack this theme, three subsequent sections look at different expressions of change: (a) seeking a better understanding of oneself, (b) setting new expectations for oneself, and (c) overcoming being underchallenged.

Better Understanding of Oneself

In this section, the common thread is that alumni reported learning about themselves due to the influence of their doctoral education experiences. Participant (A13) argued that doctoral education

> turned a lot of my preconceived ideas about learning and about myself on its ear. There were so many times where I had been strident in my opinions and then was forced to admit to myself and others that I was wrong and I really didn't know what I was talking about.

When asked to provide an example of this, alumnus (A13) stated,

> The instructors had always talked about self-as-instrument: that you really have to tap into yourself, and you really have to understand yourself, be self-aware before you can really work with anybody else. And I thought, "Oh, yeah, blah, blah, blah." But I realized as part of this one class, that it was really at the core of everything; and so that was a total awakening for me, and the turning on its ear of something that I had held true for thirty years working. In my professional background, it was all about the client ... what I thought or how I felt or how I approached things really didn't matter. So that was super exciting; to come from one position and hold it so stridently and then, through the process of working with others, of learning—of learn-

ing about myself, and learning about learning—I changed. The entire process was transformational; even when I didn't intend that or want that.

The previous quote highlighted the upending of assumptions that this person held on to for many years. Transformation around the idea of "self-as-instrument" was not intended or wanted, and yet it happened. Participant (A3) spoke about the inner change that occurred while being a doctoral student:

> it was a *huge* personal transformation. The program is very adamant about developing reflective practitioners; and I wouldn't say we were forced necessarily, but each of the courses involved a significant component around personal reflection. By taking advantage of that, it was a huge growth opportunity and really life transforming.... And the opportunity to make time for personal reflection really provided me insights into what makes me tick and how I work with others.

The quote from alumnus (A13) highlighted transformation happening without purposeful intent on the part of the student, whereas the quote from respondent (A3) underscored the deliberate cooperation with the personal-reflection assignments given by the faculty and the transformation that occurred as a result within the student. However, the common notion is that each of these graduates learned more about themselves as a result of their educational experiences. Alumnus (A20) gave an example of a specific assignment that provided the opportunity for growth in self-knowledge. Participant (A20) stated,

> I have always known on the surface what my values were, but this required us to write them down and to really think about what are the core values that we walk around with. That's something that the whole program required: a lot of reflection. But this one course required it in a more personal level, and I found that really rewarding. I mean, I have always had a kind of personal reflective quality, but this was one where I guess I had never really taken the time to look specifically at some of the things they asked us to look at within myself. That really helped to hone my understanding of who I am, what I believe in, and what is important to me, and that has helped me to frame what I want to do in my consulting business moving forward.

The self-knowledge gained in the process of doctoral education has allowed this person to think ahead about the next season of life armed with a better understanding of self. Participant (A8) believes that

> In a very corny way, I think that I am much more the person I was meant to be when I was born. In a very corny way because I think I have always been a scholar-practitioner. I think this allowed me to sort of put the endcap on

that with some very formative experiences that allowed me to really solidify a new mindset, find a new voice, and find a way to express it. In a really concrete way, after I left the work world, having a doctorate reopened higher education to me at the university level because I had a doctorate, and that led to what I am currently doing now. I see myself very much as a scholar-practitioner of organization development.

The confluence of transitioning out of a corporate environment and completing a doctoral degree allowed this person to reconnect with a more intellectually stimulating environment. Alumnus (A8) also spoke about the transformative process, especially concerning writing a dissertation:

There is a rich learning environment at our school that allows students to sort of reshape themselves and transform themselves. And so you are able to take various ideas and play with them and look at them from practical angles, from theoretical angles, research angles and then pick one that is really something that gravitates and resonates. And so by focusing in on my dissertation topic, I was able to really find an environment that allowed me to transform myself.

The reconnection with an intellectual arena was transformative for this individual. Alumnus (A8) continued with a realization about self:

To realize that your experiences were valid, your analytical frameworks were valid, that they really were emerging and new, that was extremely exciting, because like a lot of us, we sort of grow up in a world that doesn't really respect intellectual achievement, and it tends to sort of marginalize people into the average. And so you all of a sudden find out I really am not average; or at least not average in this way. There are things about me that really are worthy of a terminal degree.

Several alumni reported that they better understood themselves as a result of their doctoral education experience. Self-knowledge was intentionally sought by some and not by others, but all of the individuals above experienced it.

Set New Expectations

In addition to a better understanding of oneself, another theme of life change from alumni interviews is setting new expectations for oneself. The following two quotes are from individuals who both stated that they thought they would never even have been admitted into a doctoral program. After successfully completing a doctoral degree, both are wondering about what other limitations they might be putting on themselves that were not warranted. Alumnus (A27) stated,

Personally, it helped because I did something that I thought I could never do. If you would have talked to me ten years ago, I would have told you there is no way on earth that I could ever do a doctorate because I don't like writing and there is a lot of research—there is just no way. It was such a truth to me that I couldn't do it. But when I did it, it made me think personally, what are some other things that I think I can't do? And to be so wrong about yourself.

Respondent (A27) went on to talk about the new horizons that have been conquered after completing the degree. Likewise, participant (A19) stated,

I never believed that I could get into a doctoral program … I didn't believe that they would accept me. So once I got into the program, then I thought, "Oh, now I've got to do this" …. The whole intent of the program was to change our way of thinking. So professionally, it adjusted the way I was thinking about my work, but then personally, it forced me to look at the world in a different kind of way, even the way I personally respond to things. So for example, a very concrete thing that changed during this period of time—and I don't know if it was because of the doctoral program, but it happened at the same time—I became a marathon runner. I had never run before, but I was looking for opportunities to improve health while I was going to school and working. During the course of the time I was in the doctoral program, I ran numerous marathons. So even at a personal level, you start viewing yourself a little differently. If you believe you can't do something, well, is that really true? When you put your mind to it and put your effort and motivation towards it, maybe you can. If you have ever run a marathon, the way that you approach that and train for that and actually run it is sort of an overall picture of the way the doctoral program went for me … it becomes a whole approach to the way you face and look at your life going forward.

The alumni above spoke about setting new expectations for themselves and then achieving them. Whether it is literally learning to run a marathon, or figuratively running the marathon of doctoral education, these individuals are questioning the taken-for-granted assumptions that they had about themselves; they are choosing to change these assumptions and step into their new selves.

Overcoming Being Underchallenged

The previous section looked at several individuals who set new expectations for themselves as a result of their doctoral education. This section explores alumni views on overcoming being underchallenged in their work environments. Alumnus (A32) describes stepping into the academic venue after years of working in a corporate environment. Participant (A32) stated,

> From a professional perspective, I would have *never* been a professor today if I hadn't gone back to school. I did not intend on doing that transition. When I entered the program, I was in corporate and continued on the practitioner side. I had taught adjunct before, and I knew somewhere down the line that I would want to do that. I just didn't think it would happen so soon. Clearly, from a professional perspective, I would not be where I am today. I found myself from the corporate side saying, "Yeah, I have done this.... I have done this ten times. I don't know how many more times I want to do this. I want something different." The question is, what is different? Do I just want to go to another corporation? Am I going to do the same thing? Or am I trying something totally new? So this really stretched me in terms of thinking there is a whole other world out there and just to try it and experience it.

The familiar setting of the corporate environment did not excite and challenge this person any longer. The solution for this person was to move to a different environment altogether; the learning and growth with a career shift into academic work seemed to provide the outlet. Alumnus (A18) described a similar situation in the following interaction with the interviewer:

> Interviewer: In what ways did you stretch as a person and as a professional as a result of your doctoral education?
> A18: I gained a tremendous amount of confidence. The whole program stretched me as a person. It really took me to a whole other level, and in many ways, it was great. But in other ways, I far surpassed the knowledge that exists in the workplace today; and that was a struggle because I knew how it could be, and people are not there yet. So that became a challenge for me.
> Interviewer: So how have you managed that challenge?
> A18: Well, that is a great question. I am moving more into the consulting and academic area because that is where people expect more cutting-edge thinking.

Respondent (A18) identified being underchallenged in the current work setting and dealt with that lack of challenge by moving into other arenas that would allow for greater opportunity. Alumnus (A4) described another situation of being underchallenged and stated that doctoral education

> really helped me to be more of a critical thinker and not to just accept what had been done and what others did, and it helped me understand that if you just stop and dissect things and try and understand why people did

things, that you would start to discover things…. "I wonder why they did it that way and does that really make sense? Do I want to accept that at face value or do I want to question it?" Eventually, that led to a point where—and I guess the best way to say it—it ruined me for my position. I outgrew it. I got to a point where I felt like I was being held back, and I could apply it only so far, but when I wanted to really stretch and try new things for the division, especially when we entered into the recession … as things started to get worse, and we were laying more and more people off, I came up with an idea and went to the board and said, "You know, here is what we can do," and they just did not get it. At that point, I said, "I have to leave; I have to get out of here. I'm operating at a level where I'm questioning things that they are not willing to question." So in essence, it kind of ruined me, for it stretched me to a point where I was no more good for what I was doing.

Respondent (A4) "outgrew" the current work position and came to the conclusion that leaving it was the best solution, since people were not seeing the situation in the same manner and not listening to what (A4) offered as advice. In the following quote, participant (A12) is an individual who grew tremendously from doctoral studies in a personal way but has struggled to make the same progress in a professional context. Alumnus (A12) states,

My doctoral studies have just really expanded myself holistically. I have experienced emotional growth and of course intellectual growth and spiritual growth. I love that that's what it did. I love that I was able to really apply my learning in my personal life—emotionally and how I interact with different people—my family, my community members, and friends…. In my professional life, it is a little different because I took a leave of absence and then I ended up having to resign…. I had to go back to work or resign, and I had to get this dissertation done because so many people don't get the dissertation done…. So I haven't been able to apply and stretch into a profession yet. I haven't done that yet, and that is why I am stuck, and that is hard, and that would be one kind of loose end or a bit of a downside of the doctoral program is that it has left me—I am a little bit flailing right now. I am feeling very much adrift…. My issue right now is that I feel so chaotic because I have so many pieces now that I have learned about—now I have to try to pick up the pieces…. One small example for me is that I was so longing to get back to a work group, that I applied for my old position. I had to interview for it, and I was not selected, and it was because they said that what I have learned is—I have learned myself out of a job. I was overqualified. And I did not expect that, and well, now what? It was hard for me to realize that I was overqualified. It is an obstacle now to get back into my field the way I was … as I go on the shadow side of this is that I feel like my confidence and competence is slipping.

Respondent (A12) has not yet been able to bounce back from this new information of being "overqualified" for a job previously held. Alumnus (A12) appears to be confused and discouraged by the inability to figure out how to move forward. Some alumni were able to overcome being underchallenged in their work settings, but not all. Transitioning back into a work environment after completing a doctorate posed a challenge for all of these alumni that spoke about their experiences above.

The first section looked at important learning that occurred during doctoral education from the perspectives of alumni, as reported in their interviews. Four themes emerged from the alumni interviews. The four themes of important learning alumni highlighted are that a doctoral education (a) provided intellectual challenge, (b) instilled discipline and commitment, (c) fostered confidence and humility, and (d) promoted life change. The following section looks at the factors that inform doctoral student development as reported by alumni.

FACTORS INFLUENCING LEARNING AND DEVELOPMENT

This second main section of findings looks at the factors that inform learning and development of doctoral students as reported by alumni interviews. The backdrop is the second research question, "Do alumni see any connection between their doctoral educational experience and their own professional development, and what is the nature, if any, of this connection?" Several themes of factors surfaced that influenced doctoral student development. The six categories that describe these themes are (a) research experience, (b) engaging in new professional opportunities, (c) encouraging direct application of theory, (d) being mentored, (e) exposure and networking with leaders of the field, and (f) the richness of the cohort experience. The following section looks at the first theme.

Research Experience

Several alumni reported enjoying and benefiting from the research experience they had in their doctoral studies. Alumnus (A18) stated, "I loved the research aspect, understanding organizational culture more deeply. I was always fascinated with that, so that became something that was extremely exciting for me." In regard to qualitative research class, alumnus (A32) stated, "What really excited me was participating in it; was doing it now. I think that is what caught me. I liked the experiential piece. I really loved doing the research for my dissertation." The above respondents noted that a deeper understanding of a topic and the actual involvement in the process are two ways the research experience benefitted them. In the same vein, participant (A8) remarked,

> My dissertation was a blast. Of course, I love doing research, and I love the literature review aspect of this—I really do. I like to read and try to put together new models, and I like to actually do the research. So it was extremely exciting to work on a theoretical and take a far out theory and try to relate it to something really practical. Talking with my respondents was really a blast too. I learned a terrific amount from them.

The enthusiasm of respondent (A8) is clear; the entire challenge of the research process seemed to invigorate this person. Likewise alumnus (A6) maintained,

> I think it was exciting to see real data and how to think through theories or searches from prior research and then combine it with my own practical experience and kind of come up with some "aha" moments and validate or dismiss any perceptions I had. So I think evaluating real data that was directly related to my research, and I knew that my research was structured well because the faculty showed me how to do it correctly. So I think it was probably just reviewing the data for both the interviews and the surveys and coming up with some "aha" moments.

The excitement of this person over the research process also comes through. However, another highlight alumnus (A6) mentioned was allowing the research to challenge previously held perceptions, and as a result, this person learned new insights. Alumnus (A31) stated,

> I have never done the thematic analysis and qualitative analysis of interviews like this and text analysis to split apart what were the emerging themes that really allow you to generate insight.... And then I also learned new tricks with the whole quantitative and statistical analysis. I am not afraid of quantitative methods, having had an engineering degree and having worked in a very analytically rigorous consulting environment, but the whole structural equation modeling and way of applying quantitative methods to social sciences and really being rigorous about it allowed me to learn new skills, and now I also have an opportunity to pass that along. I run several workshops a year for the doctoral students on quantitative methods. It has given me some new skills that I can pass on to others.

Respondent (A31) gleaned new methods and ways of thinking about research from the doctorate experience that are now being used to teach others.

New Professional Opportunities

A second factor that several alumni reported as informing their development is the opening of opportunities that studying in the doctoral program created. Respondent (A35) simply stated,

> I didn't realize all of the opportunities it creates. It opens doors. I have been given opportunities with this degree to do things that I could have never done without the degree.... I can't believe the deep water that I am swimming in.

Alumnus (A15) added,

> One thing that I'd like to say about the benefits of the program and how it impacted me was that doors opened or things happened for me while I was in the program. It's not that you complete the degree and all of a sudden all of these doors open up for you. Doors opened up for me while I was in the program.

These alumni spoke of opportunities opening up during doctoral studies and after the completion of the degree. In the larger context of the interview transcripts, participant (A35) was referring to all different types of professional opportunities; whereas, alumnus (A15) spoke of opportunities in the job market. Alumnus (A8) recounted one potential avenue of contribution that professors provided to the students on a regular basis. Participant (A8) stated,

> As much as people hate our professors saying, "There is another conference coming up. Where are your submissions?" that sort of mentality is extremely helpful, and as I look back on it, I am glad that I took them up on all of those opportunities because it really socialized me into the academic community of OD & C. It got me very comfortable with figuring out ideas, working out presentations, and all that sort of thing.

Respondent (A9) also commented on the regular opportunities for participation in conferences and specifically spoke about the opportunity to present at a national conference,

> Probably the thing that stretched me the most is when we did a presentation, an all-academy presentation ... preparing, doing the research necessary, and then presenting—that was a biggie. It was like a minidissertation in itself; when you talk about the research we did, creating new models, and figuring out what was going on.

Several alumni maintained that professional opportunities were opened up during and following doctoral studies.

Direct Application of Theory

In addition to research experience and opening up opportunities, another factor that alumni named as an important piece of their development was directly applying what they learned in doctoral studies to their work environments. Alumnus (A29) simply stated, "I loved the doctoral program, and I found immediate applicability to my day-to-day work." Participant (A18) spoke specifically about the assignments:

> I thought that the assignments were all extremely relevant, and that is because I applied everything I did to my job. So because you have freedom in a doctoral program to pick your topics; and all of the subjects have relevance to the workplace. For me, I picked something that I needed to learn relative to what my job was all about.

While (A18) reported being pleased with the assignments, alumnus (A27) stated,

> I am not going to say that the whole thing captured my attention. There were some seminars that just really didn't.... But the ones that captured my attention the most were where people showed me how this worked in an organization. They would give us the theory, they would give us some examples, and then they would say this is how this actually looked on the ground. This is how we used this theory. One of my professors talks about being a scholar-practitioner all of the time. I am a practitioner-scholar. I am looking at practice first. So those classes always caught my attention more.

The seminars that had a heavier concentration on practice and showed the link to theory seemed to resonate with participant (A27). Alumnus (A15) agrees and added,

> The times when I felt most excited about it was when something that I was learning was something I could bring back to my work environment.... Situations that I felt like I could apply to my day-to-day work life I think really enthused me the most. The information that was covered was something that was very relevant to what I was doing. Something that was maybe not necessarily as relevant wasn't as exciting for me; let's say you do research classes and you know you need that to do your dissertation, but it is not something that I definitely would bring back and be able to use directly at work.

This person enjoyed the stimulation of subjects that he could easily bring back to the work environment but did not see the research classes as useful in that same environment. In contrast, participant (A1) described enjoying the challenge of attempting to bridge the theory-practice gap:

> The time I was most excited about learning was when I translated my work into research…. So the challenge comes in, how can I make this academically viable, and at the same time, drive results? It is an interesting challenge because in real life, we are mostly interested in bottom-line results—what works. In academia, we are mostly interested with what makes sense and what works. There is a focus in academia on making sense. There is a focus in the real world on what works. For me, to get the opportunity to marry the two, to make the two work together and actually accomplishing that, was very exciting.

The idea of allowing the academy and the world of practice to inform one another was exciting to the above alumnus. The give and take, back and forth seemed to be a highlight for this person. In the following statement, participant (A11) described the translation process of bringing theory into a corporate work environment. Alumnus (A11) stated,

> I was able to use real-time class discussion examples, dialogue, and bring it to my workplace within a week; sometimes OB or AI and courses around different types of change and group or interpersonal analysis. For me, working as an HR executive at the time, there was something going on in my workplace at any given time that aligned with whatever course we were doing. I would make midcourse corrections in my own work product based on things that I would learn in the program. What I would do is I would scale it to my own organization. I would take a lot of the academic words out of it. I would not go in and say, "What we first need to do is examine the micro-organizational behavior of situation" and they would be like, "What are you talking about?" So I would go in and say "Okay, I think the first step is an assessment" … and they would follow that. But I got a lot of great ideas during the cohort discussions as well as some of the facilitated discussions by the instructors and used all of the instruments as they were used and described in class.

The idea conveyed above was that this person learned from classroom interactions and study, and then the learning was almost immediately transferable into a work environment. The only caveat is that a lens of translation was employed to contextualize the information. Respondents enjoyed being able to pick topics to study that were relevant to their work. Some found the research classes to be helpful for dissertation; others enjoyed these same classes in deliberately making a step toward the interplay of theory and practice. Overall, the respondents quoted above appreciated the learning that could be directly applied to a work environment and gained insight into how theory could impact practice. Engaging in new professional opportunities and encouraging direct application of theory to work environments are two ways alumni reported learning in doctoral studies.

Being Mentored

Several alumni reported the positive benefit of being mentored by professors during their doctoral studies. Alumnus (A21) remarked,

> One of my professors was a very engaged and charismatic teacher, and I got very interested in his work. He was a great coach and mentor.... And throughout the semester, he exposed us to a variety of tools and other things for us to self-discover our own leadership strengths and weaknesses. And then at the end of the semester, he took all that data and sat down with each one of us for about two or three hours, sort of pulling it all together.

The above statement points to several aspects of mentoring: modeling being engaged in the subject matter, exposure to helpful resources, and taking the time to thoroughly debrief with the student. Another alumnus, (A18), stated,

> A18: My professors were very supportive in their own quirky way.
> Interviewer: In what ways were they supportive?
> A18: One professor was always there for me. I remember one time when I absolutely hit the wall, and I thought I could not continue on, and there was too much pressure, and this professor took me aside and was a mentor and a sage and really listened to me and helped me through. One time I turned in a really rotten paper, and he sat me down and said, "You know you are really capable of much better work, and you have to go back and rewrite this." He opened doors in certain things. I got on a professional association board because of him.... He helped me get things published.

Alumnus (A18) mentioned other aspects of mentoring: listening and effectively being present during a difficult and discouraging time for the student, challenging the student when the quality of work was subpar, and opening up doors for board appointments and publications. A highlight for respondent (A8) was "working with my dissertation committee members— one of them was extremely helpful in framing my research in a way that would get published postdissertation." Another alumnus, (A7), described the gradual building of a mentoring relationship with a professor. Respondent (A7) stated,

Knowing that I can contribute to the field, but also contribute to what I was doing in my company—I got really excited. Especially after I completed my first action research paper for a professor, and he gave me a great [job] recommendation, and he wanted me to focus on action research, and he became my mentor later on because of that.

The responses of (A8) and (A7) above both point to professors who helped the students successfully find their way through the research process with the end result of one of them being able to publish and the other affecting the practice of an organization. Alumnus (A8) elaborated,

Through this educational journey to cowrite and present with a leading OD scholar—and it gets presented by this person—that's pretty good.... To deal with somebody at the top of their field, to realize that your experiences were valid, your analytical frameworks were valid, that they really were emerging and new, that was extremely exciting.

The above quote brought another aspect of mentoring to the surface: working side-by-side together on a project with a professor. The confidence and enthusiasm that ensued in the student was clear. Alumnus (A10) highlighted one final element: modeling being a scholar-practitioner. Respondent (A10) stated,

I am proud of my ability to stand with my foot in both places [academy and practice] and there aren't many people that do. And I would say that two of my professors are the best at modeling that—they obviously come at it from the academic side; but they show up in the practitioner world, and they make their presence known in the practitioner world insomuch as they got an award for service or sharing the wealth last year at [a professional practitioner association]. So they are great models for the truly scholar-practitioner or practitioner-scholar, whichever way you want to state it. I would say they are sort of on a fulcrum.

Modeling being engaged in the subject matter, exposing students to useful resources, taking time to debrief with students, listening and giving counsel, opening up professional opportunities, providing individual guidance in the research projects, coauthoring with students, and modeling being an effective scholar-practitioner are all ways that alumni pointed out that their faculty mentored them during their doctoral studies.

Exposure and Networking With Leaders of the Field

This brief section looks at another avenue of learning mentioned by alumni: exposure and networking with leaders of the field. Alumnus

(A23) stated about the doctoral education experience, "The course track was great and the quality of the professors was excellent. The diverse makeup of the professors provided a very well-rounded education with broad exposure to perspectives in the field of study." This person found value in the diversity of the local full-time faculty, whereas alumnus (A1) spoke about visiting professors who would come to the campus and stated, "The other time I was excited about learning is really when you sit down and listen to some of the qualified dignitaries that the school was able to bring; so people who came and shared their wisdom and knowledge and opened my eyes to new perspectives." In a similar vein, alumnus (A9) stated,

> What I think was wonderful was the school brought in the rock stars of OD, and you spent time with a well-known scholar, and this person is playing the jazz piano and having a laid-back conversation like a human being.... It really gives depth. It is not just reading dry two-dimensional material—you are reading it and also thinking about the people you've connected with.

The visiting faculty took the time to engage socially with students, and this added a personal element of interaction that was meaningful to the above respondent. However, alumnus (A26) stated,

> I think the visiting faculty that come to teach are good, but I happen to believe that there is more need for mentoring and continued involvement than just star appearances that makes people improve. You know how they say with the 360 feedback—if you just give the feedback and you don't have the mentoring to follow through, it really doesn't help. I think the star appearance of leading scholars happens and then they go—it's okay, but I think that working in a long-term project or a more continued mentoring with this kind of faculty builds for a better program and better knowledge construction.

While the respondent above did find some value in being exposed to the leading scholars of the field, this person also believes the programs would be stronger with more long-term interaction and consistent mentoring.

Networking was also mentioned by alumni as a source of learning. Simply stated, alumnus (A8) remarked, "I think that the extended network of high-quality contacts within the OD community that our school has is what really, really surprised me." Respondent (A11) stated,

> I expanded my professional network beyond the core group of people that I had traditionally followed in my hometown. Because my entire twenty-year work career had been at that point building progressively responsible roles; in my hometown, I pretty much had ten or fifteen people I would bounce

things off—all there. Now I have people outside in various industries and it was great because … the collaborations began in terms of articles or let's partner around this workshop. Let's do this together. I am going to stop by your office next week when I am there for a meeting—so then this person gets to meet my coworkers and I am meeting their coworkers. And we start this multidisciplinary industry team to look at these issues, and it continues to grow even today.

The impact of building a broader collaborative professional network is what was in view in this previous statement. This brief section has looked at how alumni have learned and developed as a result by exposure and networking with leaders in the field.

The Cohort Experience

The final factor influencing learning and development named by doctoral alumni was the experiences that they had with their cohorts. Many alumni spoke about the importance of the cohort for a variety of different reasons. Five themes emerged from the alumni interviews with regard to their cohort experiences. The five themes are (a) dialogue and debate, (b) diversity, (c) building relationships, (d) effective collaboration, and (e) grieving the loss of the cohort experience.

Dialogue and Debate

One element that several alumni spoke about was their enjoyment of the interaction with their cohorts. Alumnus (A18) stated, "I loved the dialogue and debate in the class that we would have—and sometimes we took on some of the professors." Participant (A12) agreed, "The cohort experience was great. My ability to learn from all of these other perspectives was just really just a gift." Respondent (A2) was "most excited about learning" when

in the classroom, with your colleagues, and it was the enlightenment that came about because of new insights that were generated from the dialogue. So it wasn't the facilitation of the faculty, it was the cohort and the interaction amongst the cohort members that generated new energy and insights. It was a common situation that existed week after week, and so it wasn't one episode, it was just the structural element of the learning process.

According to the above statement, it was the interaction with peers in the cohort, not the facilitation of the faculty, that "generated new energy and insights" on a regular basis. Alumnus (A13) spoke about the mutual shaping effect of the cohort members. In regard to the cohort experience respondent (A13) maintained,

> I would like to think that not only has it shaped me, but I helped shape it. As a committed part of the cohort, I contributed to the group, and I helped shape the cohort. I helped shape the coursework by being honest and open and committed. I think it was absolutely a circle—there were so many dynamics. I gave back. I got a lot out of it. I gave to individuals, to parts of groups, to specific classes, to the instructors. I think I gave back to my chair—maybe not as much as my chair gave me, but I think it was a real commitment.

Alumnus (A13) pointed to the give-and-take of the cohort experience and the doctoral experience in general. The dialogue and debate in the cohort energized people, gave them new insights, and had a mutual shaping effect on the members. Another theme that alumni spoke about was the benefit derived from being in close contact with a diverse group of people.

Diversity

The diversity of the cohorts was one element that alumni pointed to that influenced their learning. Alumnus (A23) stated, "The interaction with a rich and diverse cohort of students and professors was especially exciting.... Their thoughts and ideas helped me to see the subjects from new perspectives and develop more fully through the doctoral experience." Participant (A14) agreed, "Learning from my classmates was a huge part of the learning experience. For one thing, there were people from all over the world, so I learned about areas of the world that I didn't know much about." Exposure to people from other parts of the world was a big part of this person's learning, according to the previous statement. In addition to cultural diversity, alumnus (A11) spoke about another type of difference in the cohort:

> The richness of the discussion; what I walked away with each classtime was many different perspectives from across the country, various industries, to the same problem. Listening to how they would solve this OD intervention within academia, health care, consulting.... Not that the instructors were not great. They were, but I was used to instructors. The instructors were doing what I was accustomed that instructors would do. They are teaching and guiding and facilitating discussion. What I never ever experienced before was the amount of growth and knowledge that I would take place from peers and classmates. In a traditional program, you just don't focus there, and now if I were to quickly jot down all of my "take-aways" from the program; I really can't tell you how many came from classmates and how many were from formalized instruction.

Alumnus (A11) appreciated the diversity of backgrounds and industries that were represented in the cohort. Much of the learning was attributed to the interactions of the classmates, and this was somewhat surprising to this individual. Participant (A32) pointed out a different element that was surprising about interacting with the cohort. Alumnus (A32) stated,

> It was so diverse in the cohort. We weren't all from the same background. People brought so many perspectives to the table. Everybody was engaged and was able to participate and took every other person there seriously. We shared a lot of information, and to me, that was extremely important. I think that one of the things that caught on to me about the academic world is that you just share information. The whole intent of going through a dissertation, of going through that process is that I am going to put it out there to share, to learn from this, and maybe they will take it one step further. I think that whole process for me is very intriguing. One of the other key points that I wanted to bring up was the exposure to so many different people—academic people as well as practitioner people with so many different backgrounds. The program allowed us that opportunity, and I don't think that if I had not been in the program, I would have made those kinds of contacts.

This respondent appreciated the diversity of perspectives and the respectful way each person was heard in the cohort. However, the thing that was surprising to this person was the sharing of information and the priority placed upon that within the academy. It seemed that the diversity in the group made this sharing of information all the more rich. The realization was also shared that meeting this group of diverse people might not have happened had it not been for the doctoral program. In summary, new perspectives were gained by cohort members due to the cultural diversity and the wide range of backgrounds and industries represented.

Building Relationships

Another element that alumni brought up was the importance of the relationships that were built in their cohorts. Regarding the cohort, alumnus (A7) stated, "The network was amazing. I stay in touch with a lot of people. I consider them close friends and family." Alumnus (A1) also pointed to the importance of the relationships:

> The other time I was excited about learning is when we met as a cohort. Listening to the stories of other students, to their struggles, to their accomplishments, also was exciting. The social interacting of the cohort, the friendships that evolved.... It wasn't always about the knowledge, sometimes it was about the new relationships that we developed.

The social aspect of the cohort relationships was important to participants (A7) and (A1). Respondent (A10) went out of the way to talk about the cohort experience:

> The one thing that we haven't talked about that I would be remiss in not mentioning in that had it a significant influence on me was the cohort of people that I went through it with. That fifty percent of the experience was just what I experienced with the cohort—nothing to do with the education—we could have been studying zoology—who knows. But fifty percent of it was the cohort experience and the support and camaraderie and experiences that we went through over those three years together. Fifty percent of it was personal effort and whatever else that was outside of it might have actually been coursework and everything else. And obviously that is kind of a little facetious because the coursework and the structure provided the framework for that to happen.

This alumnus went on to say that this particular doctoral program was chosen because of the regular face-to-face interaction that was part of the structure of the experience. Alumnus (A3) stated the opposite:

> I went into the program in spite of the fact that it was cohort based. I didn't want to do anything to do with a cohort. I always saw myself as a lone wolf. Group projects were always a pain in the ###. Just let me do my thing and enjoy this and don't make me have to interact with a lot of other people. What I discovered was that the cohort was *extremely* important, and I developed lifelong friends. And I am not one that makes a lot of friends—I just don't. I am very careful and very selective about the friends that I make, but I would say there isn't a person in my cohort that I wouldn't give my left arm for when they needed it. So it was really transformative in that respect in terms of developing relationships with others and very deep relationships, certainly not casual at all.

Initially, this person was averse to interacting in a cohort, but over time, participant (A3) warmed up to and embraced the familial aspect of the cohort. Building relationships is an important supportive element of the learning process in the doctoral experience.

Effective Collaboration

Previous statements above speak about cohort members sharing insights and knowledge, support and camaraderie, and a mutual shaping of one another. This brief section looks at the collaboration of cohort members. Alumnus (A13) gave a specific example:

> There was one group experience that stands out in my mind as being the perfect coming together of topic and people and energy and commitment—

all the things I value. It was a paper that we were supposed to put together and do research on, and there were three people in the group including me, and we all had totally diverse backgrounds, and we just enjoyed each other, and we all worked equally and energetically toward a common goal. There was a personal crisis of one of the people during that time, and she was still so committed to us that she made sure that she showed her commitment even while she was going through something really difficult with her family. It was one of the more energizing experiences in my life, and the three of us still talk about it as—wouldn't it be great if it was always like that. That was just a peak experience for the relationships and the learning and doing something that none of us really knew all that much about.... We sensed a certain kind of kindred spirit in the way we worked, and that was really wonderful, and so we used all of our individual skills, and yet we took some risks in doing some things that we weren't that skilled at—it was safe and it was fun. It was one of the few times in my life where I wasn't so individually focused, that I was really committed to the group and having the team do well. That was pretty new for me—I've never been like that.

The effective collaboration mentioned above was attributed to several factors: a common goal, equal work load, energy toward the goal, a kindred spirit, using individual skills, taking risks, and a commitment to the well-being of the group. Alumnus (A14) described a different type of collaboration experience:

Our program is very intense.... And for me, it was even more intense because I was an anomaly in the group. Everybody else was coming from a big organization; I wasn't. And also, everybody else had international experience; I didn't. So I was not only learning the curriculum, but I was catching up to the others. So for me, it was a constant learning path.... When I was learning statistics—I have never taken a statistics course. Again, I was the only one that hadn't. And I was very nervous about it. For the beginning of the statistics classes, I was behind, but by about the middle of the class it became a new type of statistics and nobody knew it. So I was more on an even playing field, but what I found was that we worked together, and it was amazing to be part of the cohort. The people were so interesting. They were high achievers. They were so smart, so experienced but willing to share their experience and willing to explore together. They never shut me out, and that was really very important. It was important especially to me because I was an outsider, and they helped me be part of the group.... I don't know if I could have made it through the program without the support of my classmates. I'm sure I wouldn't have, in fact. But I have to tell you, when it came to statistics, I did reach a level where I was actually helping others. So others felt that way about me too, eventually. Not at first, but eventually.

The above statement highlights other aspects of collaboration: willingness to share and explore, inclusion of each member, support, and receiving and giving help when needed. The final quote of this section points to the postdoctorate collaboration of a cohort. Alumnus (A1) stated,

> Actually, we even engaged in some work together. With one of the members we coauthored a paper, and now we are working in coauthoring a book. Other members, we are in constant communication, and of course the social media makes this even easier. Those of us who use Facebook are probably in touch with each other more than others.

Collaboration continued beyond the doctoral degree for the alumni quoted above.

Grieving the Loss of the Cohort Experience

The final theme that emerged from the alumni interviews was the feelings of loss and frustration after completing the coursework with structured cohort meetings and moving into the isolation of the dissertation phase. Alumnus (A12) stated,

> I talk to my cohort and colleagues and we all kind of say that—you get done with the comps, oral and written, and we are *really* out on our own. The cohort model is so supportive, and we love each other so much, and then you are separated—just like that—cut. And the dissertation thing is so individualized and isolating and time-consuming; and then when you are done with that, you are trying to reconnect, and it's hard because life is busy.

The loss of the supportive familial relationships that had been such a part of the learning environment during the coursework was now severed or "cut," and this seemed to intensify the feelings of isolation. Alumnus (A20) recounted a similar experience:

> One of the things that struck me, and the professors probably tried to prepare us for this, but I don't really remember it. When our classes ended, then you take your comprehensive exams, and then there are no more cohort meetings, or residencies. And then you work on the dissertation. They gave us a lot of things in that last residency about the dissertation process and how to write a proposal, but then you are kind of left on your own, and it seemed like all support networks were kind of ended. Unless we decided to keep in touch with certain people in our cohort, which I think we had pretty much done, then we are kind of left there out on our own and some people still struggling with their proposal. It is like "Okay, now you are on your own." The faculty is available if we want to meet with them, but it seems like there is something missing in that transition.... If there is something that could be incorporated into that transition, or is there a way to make it a little more formal in terms of forming a study group or getting people to buddy up or getting them to get in touch with someone who has completed a dissertation to help them

through some of that initial stuff to help coach them through it or do something, because I think people get lost in that.

The difficulty mentioned in leaving the support of the cohort was similar to the first account, and this alumnus went on to offer suggestions to put something in place that would make the transition easier. Respondent (A15) added to the theme,

> What was really a stretch for me, which I didn't anticipate at all, was completing the dissertation. It just seemed like in the doctoral program we were all together there as a cohort. We went through our comprehensives, and we had our last meeting where we got together, and we were talking about our dissertations and working on our topics or proposals; and then, everybody went in different directions and never came back again. I feel like that was a challenge, and I feel like if we would have come back, it could have been part of the program to come back maybe on a regular basis, maybe monthly check in or a quarterly check in. People could talk about where they are at and share ideas.... The struggle for me was we went off on our own directions and from there, life happened, and it was a real challenge to prioritize the schoolwork over life and work. I made a job change during that time and other things happened. It actually took me four years. There are a lot of changes that people encounter in four years of their life, obviously. That was a real challenge for me to get through that.... I really had to be persistent with it. I will be honest, there were several times where I thought, just chuck this thing because it was like a monkey on your back. But I didn't want to invest that much time and effort into something and not finish it. I know from talking to other people in the cohort, they encountered the same thing, and there are other people still working on it. I feel like it has been a struggle for many people.

This respondent admitted to having great difficulty in completing the dissertation without the network of the cohort as a support. The final quote looks at this loss from a different angle. Alumnus (A19) stated,

> You know you have this intense cohort process.... And there is sort of this replenishing of relationships and so on; but when the classwork was done, you would go into this solitary yearlong effort when you are working on your dissertation. But then it is over, and you try to maintain contact/connection with the students you were working with, and you can do it with some but not with others. The social thing has changed—the social learning has changed, and also the structure that the program provided in terms of promoting learning and so on has changed as well. I think every student faces that issue. So there is nothing to be changed within the educational piece or the structure itself, but I think what happens afterwards—what is postdoctoral life looking like? Also, every doctoral student faces that. For some people, there is a tremendous sense of relief that they can go on with

their life. But if you love learning, if you are curious, if you love to spend time with people who are thinking about the same kind of stuff you are thinking about everyday; it is a community that kind of dissolves over time, and that can be difficult.

This alumnus did not report problems with the sense of loss in the dissertation phase of study; the sense of loss appeared afterward when people had completed that phase and it was difficult to stay connected. The sense of vacancy that this person felt was clear. The richness of the cohort experience seemed to be felt as a significant loss once it was formally over. Five themes emerged from the alumni interviews with regard to their cohort experiences. The five themes are (a) dialogue and debate, (b) diversity, (c) building relationships, (d) effective collaboration, and (e) grieving the loss of the cohort experience.

In summary, several themes of factors surfaced that influenced doctoral student learning development as reported by alumni. Six categories encompass the themes. The six categories that described these themes were (a) research experience, (b) engaging in new professional opportunities, (c) encouraging direct application of theory, (d) being mentored, (e) exposure and networking with leaders of the field, and (f) the richness of the cohort experience. The following segment looks at the last section of findings based on alumni interviews.

CONTRIBUTIONS TO THE FIELD

The two sections of findings reported thus far in this chapter are the important learning themes and the factors influencing learning and development. The final section of findings from alumni interviews looks at what alumni report as their contributions to the field. The findings take their cue from the third research question: "What do doctoral alumni identify as their most important contributions to the field of OD or management?" Three themes of contribution to the field surfaced from the interviews with alumni. The three themes were making contributions through publishing, through practice, and through building into the lives of the next generation of leaders. The following sections explore these themes, as well as a final section reporting the findings from the curriculum vitae and résumés that each alumnus submitted prior to the interview.

Publishing

One of the contributions alumni reported was publishing literature in the field. Several individuals mentioned their dissertation as a contribution that they had made to the field. However, below are a few examples of what graduates said about their publishing accomplishments other than completing the dissertation. Alumnus (A18) maintained as a result of doctoral education, "I have been doing a lot of publishing. I am writing a book." Respondent (A2) stated, "I have written two chapters and two books and I have published a major article in an international journal and my dissertation." Alumnus (A8) reported, "I have a few publications out there. I think I have done a pretty good job of furthering the discussion on my topic. I am very frustrated that it hasn't gone any further than that." Participant (A7) believes that

> As a professional, the doctorate gave me more credibility.... I have written things that have been published that I do not think would have been published if I did not have a doctorate because I tried to publish articles before I got my doctorate, and often got rejected, but the same papers submitted later with a doctorate by my name provided that access.

Alumnus (A9) stated that the biggest contribution made was in writing a book that was practical and not "heavy PhD-level reading; that I am really proud of probably the most, and then miscellaneous articles." Many people mentioned things other than publishing as their most significant contribution; the following sections will explore a couple of these.

Practice

Two avenues of contribution were named related to practice: (a) a dual role of scholar and practitioner, and (b) helping "my organization."

Dual Roles

Only a couple of alumni specifically mentioned that their contribution to the field is in being a scholar-practitioner. Alumnus (A8) admitted, "I see myself very much as a scholar-practitioner of organization development." Alumnus (A1) plainly stated, "I think that I join the list of other scholar-practitioners.... I think that I continue to contribute to the field, being able to live in both worlds." And respondent (A10) maintained,

> I would never call myself an academic because I don't live in that realm ... but I have definitely planted a solid foot in the scholarly world enough to be able to stand, to be able to stand between the two and draw the best of both back and forth, which is extremely exciting for me and a place that I didn't stand before.

Pride regarding the ability to be a scholar-practitioner shines through in the statement made by participant (A10).

Home-Base Organization

Several alumni mentioned that the contribution to the field they are making was to help their home-base organizations. Five brief examples are given below. Alumnus (A1) stated, "I contributed to my own organization in providing ideas and guidance and what could be the best way to move forward that is helpful." In the same vein, respondent (A23) maintained, "My new education helped me improve the efficiency of my organization through the application of a more theoretical understanding of the business." Likewise, alumnus (A15) stated, "I guess contributing in the work I do here at my organization and applying the things that I learned in the doctoral program here and making this a more effective organization overall or at least within my department." Participant (A23) reported, "My most significant contributions were invested in my company, applying multiple perspectives on organizational theory in harmony with my many years of business experience." Alumnus (A6) maintained, "I probably helped … in a broader organizational perspective, just helping the company improve at customer service and increase overall productivity in the workforce." Alumni mentioned several ways in which their doctoral education prepared them to make a contribution to their home-base organizations: provided ideas and guidance, increased efficiency and effectiveness, applied theory to business setting, improved customer service and increased productivity.

Develop the Next Generation

A third theme that emerged from alumni interviews regarding their contributions to the field was the notion of developing the next generation of leaders. Some alumni believe their role is developing students in an academic environment, while others use their home-base organizations or professional associations to develop the next generation. Alumnus (A2) argued,

I am not into research. I don't see sitting behind a computer generating data every day is my forte, if I was forty years of age maybe I would do that, but I am sixty, so I see my role as being in the classroom and sharing what I can with new students coming up that will make an impression on the world.

Likewise, participant (A27) stated,

If there were a contribution that I was proud of, I would say it is that I have taught other people. I have been teaching about ten years now. And I get calls from students all the time asking me questions about a project or telling me about what happened with a project—just to affect that many different people—it is really cool, and I get so much satisfaction out of that.

On the practitioner side of the equation, alumnus (A6) stated, "I probably helped a lot of folks that have worked for me come out of their shell and accomplish things and feel good about themselves and develop confidence that they might not have otherwise had." Respondent (A10) spoke about making other types of opportunities for the next generation. Alumnus (A10) stated,

> I am more concerned about insuring that there are opportunities for other people and doing it in places where I feel there is opportunity for impact. So being able to be in a role of mentor or coach or support other people as they grow has always been my mode of operating and will continue to be. And I feel fortunate enough, I mean, I am not that old that I have had a lot of younger folks that I have been able to help to kind of shepherd along the way and obviously people in the doctoral program that I have been able to be helpful to as a peer. So *that* is where I am most proud of my contribution; is to engage other people's work so that they can make a contribution and there is no A, B, or C way to do it.

Last, respondent (A23) believes, "My doctoral education has instilled within me a greater responsibility toward other people and how to contribute to society as a whole beyond simply conducting a business." Clearly, these individuals are concerned about building into the lives and practice of the next generation of leaders. They all see it as a significant contribution to the field.

Three themes of contribution to the field surfaced from the interviews with alumni. The three themes were making contributions through publishing, through practice, and through building into the lives of the next generation of leaders. Ironically, five of the alumni interviewed stated that they did not believe they had made any significant contributions to the field of OD or management at all.

Curriculum Vitae and Résumés

This brief section highlights the data from the alumni curriculum vitae, résumés, and short biographies. All of the participants were asked to supply a curriculum vitae or résumé prior to their scheduled interview. The breakdown was as follows: curriculum vitae (24 participants), résumés that were shorter than two pages (6 participants), short biographies that were under one page (4 participants), and one person who did not comply. To be clear, only 35 alumni volunteered written information about their personal histories.[1] Given that some of the personal histories on the CVs were as long as 40 pages and some of the short bios were as brief as 250 words, running any type of statistical comparison would not be appropriate. A few findings can be gleaned from these self-reported documents.

Years of Professional Service

A brief summary of the findings on the group of alumni are given in this section. Close to 1,000 years of professional service has been accumulated by this group of individuals. The data broke naturally into three groups:

- People with under 20 years of experience (5 alumni)
- People with 20 to 29 years of experience (18 alumni)
- People with over 30 years of experience (11 alumni)

The mean average was 27.1, median 25, mode 25, and range 32. The least amount of professional experience was 12 years and the most was 44 years.

Industries and Professional Positions

Many different industries are represented in this group. Some of them include retail management, health care, information technology, telecommunications, aerospace, higher education, criminal justice, and assorted nonprofits. All but one alumnus reported having experience in some type of management. Many of these individuals hold executive or senior management positions. Some of their titles include Chief Executive Officer/President, Chief People Officer, Chief Learning Officer, Chief Operating Officer, Chief Medical Officer, Chief Human Resources Officer, Executive Vice-President, Director of Global OD, Director of Marketing, Regional Project Managers, Principal Consultant, Assistant and Associate Professors, and Business Owner. Of all of the 36 alumni, only 5 are full-time faculty. Three of the five alumni that are now full-time faculty reportedly made the switch from a corporate environment to higher education either during or just following the completion of their doctoral education. Of the alumni that work in full-time corporate jobs, 19 also work as adjunct faculty in various universities alongside their full-time employment.

Academic Contributions and Publishing Records

While some of the résumés and short bios did not report any publications due to the brevity of the document, many of the CVs and résumés did document publishing records. Note was made by 25 individuals of some type of peer-reviewed publishing on their respective documents. Many listed presentations, panels, service to the academy, and awards that they had won. Report was made by 20 of the alumni as being members of the Academy of Management. Some of these individuals served as Academy of

Management paper reviewers and in leadership positions as well. Membership and leadership in other professional and academic associations were noted by these same individuals.

In summary, three sections of findings were reported based on interviews with doctoral graduates. The three sections of findings were (a) important learning, (b) factors influencing learning and development, and (c) self-reported contributions to the field.

NOTE

1. The person who declined stated that the CV was out-of-date and would not reflect an accurate picture.

CHAPTER 7

A SYNTHESIS OF FINDINGS

The focus of this chapter is to converge the research findings and precedent literature into a synergetic discussion. Three broad arenas will be explored: the learning, the educational framework, and the contributions of the alumni.

THE LEARNING

The overarching question of this segment is "Did the intended learning outcomes of the faculty actually align with what alumni reported that they learned?" One realizes that the faculty did not have the time to exhaustively articulate all of their learning outcomes; however ample opportunity was given for them to communicate the most important outcomes. The line of questioning that provided the best opportunity resided in two of the interview questions: "What are you most hopeful that students will learn from being in this program?" and "In addition to what you just mentioned, are there any other primary learning outcomes that you desire for students in this program?" The hope in asking these questions was that the faculty would name the learning outcomes that they are most passionate about and what they wanted to make sure that students understood and embraced before they completed the degree. Thus, the connotation of the term "learning outcomes" used here,

> Reflects a conceptual shift towards making learning more meaningful and effective for students. It mostly refers to the qualitative outcomes of student

Educating the Scholar Practitioner in Organization Development, pp. 105–115 learning which emphasize understanding and obtaining meaning rather than quantitative outcomes of learning which have a focus on acquisition of factual knowledge. (Varnava-Marouchou, 2009, p. 98)

Likewise, the graduates did not have enough time in the interview to address all of the learning that took place in their doctoral education experience. Yet several opportunities were given for alumni to voice their perceptions about their significant learning. Three questions aimed at the idea of learning: "Looking back at your doctoral education experience, could you tell me about a time when you were most excited about learning?" "In what ways did your doctoral education stretch you as a person and as a professional?" and "How do you believe you have changed as a result of your doctoral education?" The hope was that they would highlight what was most meaningful or engaging and what had the greatest impact on them both personally and professionally.

With that information as a backdrop, the question remains, Did the intended learning outcomes of the faculty actually align with what alumni reported that they learned? The learning that faculty members intended and the learning that influenced alumni did converge in certain places. However, in other places, alumni learning appeared to diverge from the intended learning outcomes, exposing some of the potential hidden curriculum of these programs. The term "hidden" does not connote a secret agenda on the part of the faculty to accomplish an outcome. Rather, hidden curriculum simply means "a broad category that includes all of the unrecognized and sometimes unintended knowledge, values, and beliefs that are part of the learning process in schools and classrooms" (Horn, 2003, p. 298). In other words, alumni learning went beyond the intended learning outcomes that were stated by the faculty.

What follows in this section is the juxtaposition of intended learning outcomes reported by the faculty, the alumni reflections that correspond to these outcomes (if any), and pertinent literature on the subject. Four specific learning outcomes will be raised in this section.[1] The four learning outcomes are research capabilities, knowledge of the field of OD, self-development, and critical thinking.[2]

Research Capabilities

Some of the learning outcomes that the faculty articulated in the interviews were anticipated. For example, the attainment of basic competencies is a standard learning outcome at the graduate level of study (James & Brown, 2005). For the doctoral student, a basic competency is developing the mindset and skills of a researcher (Gilbert, 2009). As previously mentioned, important learning outcomes for doctoral students revolve around research capabilities, making an "original contribution (new facts or knowledge, formulating theories, reinterpreting data or ideas)," "implementing research project," "critical review of literature of field," "methodological techniques and skills," "independent critical thought," "relevance to scholarship in the field," "formulating problems," and "research ethics" (p. 61). Golde (2006) and others put emphasis on students being inculcated as stewards of the discipline; it is not surprising that research capabilities were mentioned in the interviews with faculty as an important learning outcome.

Several alumni mentioned they were energized by the research component of doctoral education. The new set of skills and research experience base benefited them. The individuals who appeared to embraced and internalize this researcher mindset saw that these abilities would be useful going forward in their professional contexts. Other alumni were not as excited about the research aspects of the degree, but did see the necessity of research capabilities to write the dissertation and be able to read literature intelligently. Some alumni made no comment with regard to learning research methodology.

A hidden curriculum seems to be associated with the rigors of research. Several alumni connected growth in discipline and commitment to the challenge of doctoral research and completing the dissertation research project. Two metaphors of physical exertion that alumni used to describe the diligent challenge of doctoral education were "three years of weight lifting" (A10) and "running a marathon" (A19); these metaphors seem to be an attempt to illustrate the discipline, commitment, persistence, and strength it takes to complete the degree.

Knowledge of OD

Being well-versed in the main body of OD knowledge is necessary to be an effective professional in this field (Cummings & Worley, 2009). Understanding the ideas, concepts, and processes of a given field is an appropriate basic learning outcome for graduate students (Bourner, 1997; James & Brown, 2005). Knowledge of the field is essential since conservation of knowledge within one's own field of study is one of the expectations of being a steward of the discipline (Golde, 2006). It is not surprising that knowledge of the field was mentioned by faculty as important learning for students.

While alumni did not specifically mention OD knowledge base as their most important learning, they did speak about being challenged intellectually during their classroom discussions and shifting their thinking about theory and practice as a result. Similarly, graduates also spoke of the benefit of applying theory to work environments, which one could argue implies understanding and valuing the knowledge base itself.

Self-Development

The literature is straightforward; "intrapersonal skills" are vital to an OD professional (Cummings & Worley, 2009, p. 53). Similarly, a "clear knowledge of self" is necessary for the effective practice of OD (Worley & Feyerherm, 2003, p. 103). Personal development, then, is an appropriate learning outcome for graduate students (Bourner, 1997; Gilbert, 2009). Several faculty members mentioned self-development as an important learning outcome for students. According to alumni, doctoral education instilled discipline and commitment, contributed to increased confidence and humility, led to a better understanding of oneself, helped to set new expectations for oneself, and helped to overcome being underchallenged.

One avenue of self-development that was mentioned by alumni was an increase in discipline and commitment. Growth in time-management skills and priority-management abilities are examples of increased discipline that alumni spoke about in their interviews. Self-directed learning was another discipline that alumni mentioned. A quote from alumnus (A5) illustrates this point: "Doctoral education is about being self-taught. My skillset that I was there to develop is how to teach myself to learn. And I did that." Many adult educators endorse self-directed learning as an effective mode of learning for adults (Brookfield, 1990; Knowles, 1988; Vella, 1994). Planning and managing one's own learning is an appropriate graduate student learning outcome (Bourner, 1997). Successful doctoral education depends upon students growing in their "abilities and actions to be self-directed learners: being able to pursue learning beyond their mentors, engaging in critically reflective examination of knowledge and disciplinary assumptions, and to become peer scholars to their doctoral mentors" (Kasworm & Bowles, 2010, p. 225). In short, "current learning theory suggests that the key skills and attitudes of self-directed learning are pivotal for the success of adults in doctoral studies" (p. 226). Learning how to learn is the key task in becoming a self-directed learner.

Several alumni reported that their doctoral education instilled confidence, humility, or both confidence and humility. The literature mentions the possibility of graduate student learning outcomes being aimed at developing dispositions, which include attitudes, perceptions, and motivations (James & Brown, 2005). Instilling confidence and humility could be viewed as a dispositional learning outcome of self-development encouraged directly by faculty;[3] however, it more is likely that this growth is an element of hidden curriculum. According to alumni, successfully completing the rigorous challenge of a doctoral dissertation is the source of increased self-confidence. In other words, growth in a broader self-confidence seems to be a by-product of the entire research process rather than any one individual element instituted by faculty. Likewise, growth in humility may also be a hidden curriculum. Alumni point to increasing humility in light of either the stark realization of the vast amount of knowledge that is available or from rubbing shoulders with their knowledgeable cohort members, professors, and other leaders in the field.

Another learning outcome expressed by several faculty members was for students to grow in self-awareness through the desire and capacity to engage in self-reflection. Indeed, numerous alumni reported that their doctoral education led to a better self-understanding. Likewise, Harris (2007) found that doctoral students reported, as a result of their education, an increase in self-awareness through critical reflection. Disorienting dilemmas pose as catalysts for critical reflection (Mezirow, 2000).

One source of disequilibration for doctoral students is the addition of the scholar identity to their already busy lives (Austin & McDaniels, 2006). The struggle to integrate multiple identities is difficult for many students (Kasworm & Bowles, 2010). This struggle opens up the opportunity for students to critically reflect and challenge the obsolete assumptions that they carry about themselves. For example, as a result of completing the doctoral degree, alumni in this study who had thought they could never accomplish this goal were forced to reevaluate that assumption, and through critical reflection decided to challenge other constraining assumptions and set additional new expectations for themselves as a result. For doctoral students, "integrating all the professional identities" is an important process to enhance their "productivity, time and energy management, and well-being" (Colbeck, 2008, p. 13).

Similarly, for some alumni, the discontentment with being underchallenged at work provided a catalyst to critically reflect, challenge assumptions, and take action to change the situation. Transformative learning theory would argue that the next phases after exploring new options and roles would be to plan a course of action, acquire necessary skills to implement the plan, try on the new role, and build competence and confidence in the new role (Mezirow, 2000). Colbeck (2008) observes, "Once an individual has accepted and internalized expectation for a role as part of his or her identity, that identity becomes a cognitive framework for interpreting new experiences" (p. 10). Several examples exist in the stories of alumni that highlight making a shift to a new role that allows for a more authentic expression of personhood in their work environment or perhaps changing their work environment. These examples align with the three factors named in the literature that promote professional development: individuation, authenticity and transformative learning (Cranton & King, 2003). However, one alumnus (A12) openly shared about the struggle brought on through doctoral education:

> So I haven't been able to apply and stretch into a profession yet. I haven't done that yet, and that is why I am stuck, and that is hard, and that would be one kind of loose end or a bit of a downside of the doctoral program is that it has left me—I am a little bit flailing right now. I am feeling very much adrift.... My issue right now is that I feel so chaotic because I have so many pieces now that I have learned about—now I have to try to pick up the pieces.... One small example for me is that I was so longing to get back to a work group, that I applied for my old position. I had to interview for it, and I was not selected, and it was because they said that what I have learned is— I have learned myself out of a job. I was overqualified. And I did not expect that, and well, now what? It was hard for me to realize that I was overqualified. It is an obstacle now to get back into my field the way I was ... as I go on the shadow side of this is that I feel like my confidence and competence is slipping.

Respondent (A12) has been living in the middle of a disorienting dilemma and appears to be confused and discouraged by the inability to figure out how to move forward. This illustrates the considerable pressure for personal change and the "risk of losses of the self" associated with doctoral education (Kasworm & Bowles, 2010, p. 233).

Critical Thinking

Several faculty members mentioned the ability to think critically as an essential learning outcome for doctoral students. In the literature, a general learning outcome for graduate students is higher-order learning and the use of critical faculties, such as advanced thinking, reasoning, or metacognition (Bourner, 1997; James & Brown, 2005). Doctoral students need to be able to produce "independent critical thought" (Gilbert, 2009, p. 61) or the "cognitive and creative construction of meaning and generation of ideas" (Bourner, 1997; James & Brown, 2005). The ability to think critically is aimed at making an original contribution to the knowledge base (Gilbert, 2009). This learning outcome seems to be met as alumni specifically described increased ability to think critically, shifts in their thinking about important topics, and a broadening of their perspectives.

THE EDUCATIONAL FRAMEWORK

The framework through which the learning takes place is the theme of this second segment. Faculty articulated important elements regarding the teaching learning process and creating a learning environment. According to faculty, creating a learning environment involved being aware of the student's individual needs, creating a collegial ethos, the cohort model, socialization into the field, and assessment of learning.

Individual Attention

Several faculty members reported the need to pay individual attention to their doctoral students, recognizing "the graduate as the 'knowing subject' of doctoral work" (Lee & Boud, 2009, p. 19). The individual attention happened through listening, counseling, mentoring and not "giving up on people easily" (F6). Giving individual attention to students supports a learner-oriented environment. As stated above, the importance of a learner-oriented environment is crucial in adult education (Boyatzis, Cowen, & Kolb, 1995; Brookfield, 2005; Brookfield & Preskill, 1999; Freire, 1997; Knowles, 1988; Schön, 1987; Vella, 1995).

The study of Harris (2007) highlights that informal mentoring by faculty leads to growth in the students. Likewise in this study, as a factor that influenced their learning, alumni mentioned that being mentored by faculty was an important element. Some of the examples of mentoring that took place are modeling being engaged in the subject matter, exposure to helpful resources, listening and effectively being present during a difficult and discouraging time for the student, challenging the student when the quality of work was subpar, helping the student successfully find their way through the research process with the end results of both knowledge generation and improved practice, opening up new professional opportunities for professional advancement such as board appointments or coauthoring publications with students.

Creating a Collegial Ethos

A collegial ethos involves building an environment where students can be creators of knowledge and not "consumers of already-packaged knowledge" (F4). Students are treated as contributing and respected professionals whose work is worthy of being built upon. The seminar format of teaching allows the students to study ahead of time and come to the class time prepared to dialogue with the professor and the other participants around the subject matter.

Alumni did not specifically mention the egalitarian environment as a factor that influenced their learning. This is not to say that the collegial ethos was not appreciated or that it did not contribute to their learning; rather, the presence of it may have been a tacit type of factor that did not explicitly become articulated. The collegial nature of the process could potentially be evidenced in the increase of both confidence and humility on the part of the alumni: confidence in the sense that they learn to state their opinions in a collegial open environment and humility in the sense that the alumni are surrounded by other very capable people, and it is a reminder that one can never exhaustively know everything.

The Cohort Model

Harris (2007) states regarding doctoral learning that "the cohort itself consistently laid the foundation for growth" (p. 331). All of the programs in this study use a cohort model of education. Professors use the cohort as an ongoing way of giving shape to the educational process. Based on their interviews, faculty members were aware of the positive impact and the rich interaction that happens in these groups of students. The cohort model allows for faculty-facilitated discussion and a student-peer teaching and learning approach to doctoral education.

While the faculty members only made brief references to the cohort model as a component of the educational process, as a factor influencing learning, the cohort experience was quite significant according to alumni. When asked the interview question, "Looking back at your doctoral education experience, could you tell me about a time when you were most excited about learning?" the most common response was the intense dialogue and debate that happened in the cohort experiences. According to alumni, the diversity of the cohorts made the experience even richer. The relationships that were built in the cohort were very meaningful to the members.[4] Alumni reported effective collaboration with cohort members as a highlight. Several alumni expressed feelings of loss and frustration after completing the coursework with the structured cohort meetings and moving into the isolation of the dissertation phase. The feelings of loss further illustrate the strong bond of the cohort that was created throughout the educational process.

Socialization Into the Field

Boud and Lee (2009) state that professional research doctorates are "commonly profession-specific and are more directly aimed at midcareer professionals, or as advanced training grounds for particular professional groups" (p. 3). Part of the professional learning that takes place within advanced educational degrees is the specific processes of socialization that are unique to each field of study. In other words, socialization of students into a discipline is customary in doctoral education (Gardner & Mendoza, 2010). Socialization in graduate education affects how doctoral students see themselves, their work, what work is deemed valuable, and what it means to be a professional in their field (O'Meara, 2008). The process of socialization plays a strong role in the development of professional identity (Jebril, 2008).

The faculty spoke about socialization of students through building a connection to the profession and through providing exposure to the leaders of the field. The gradual socializing process involves easing students into doctoral studies by answering initial questions and providing useful tools and content, then eventually helping them identify their interest areas within the field, and ultimately make a contribution to the profession. A tangible connection to the field happens as a result of participation in the academic and professional conferences. James and Brown (2005) speak about socialization as a learning outcome of "membership, inclusion, and self-worth" (p. 10). Some alumni did feel the socializing pressure from the faculty. Participant (A8) stated,

> As much as people hate our professors saying, "There is another conference coming up. Where are your submissions?" that sort of mentality is extremely helpful, and as I look back on it, I am glad that I took them up on all of those opportunities because it really socialized me into the academic community of OD & C. It got me very comfortable with figuring out ideas, working out presentations, and all that sort of thing.

The other avenue of socialization was through exposure to leaders in the field. Faculty member (F4) plainly stated that, "One of the big ways that students are socialized into the field is that we bring in ... the recognized leaders in the field ... giving the students access to the people who are the pioneers and the leading edge of the field." Several alumni mentioned the exposure to the thought leaders and leading practitioners was a time they were "most excited about learning."

Assessment of Learning

Three elements of assessment were briefly mentioned: reflective integrative assignments, practical assignments, and the dissertation. Several faculty use reflective integrative assignments. The work of Schön (1983) on the "reflective practitioner" informs some of the philosophy and assignments given by several faculty members, whereas professor (F13) "provokes" students in order to cause self-reflection, discernment, and articulation of their own unique personal vision. In either case, the alumni seem to benefit from the imposition of self-reflection assignment. Even some of the more reluctant alumni admit they have benefited from the reflective assignments. Alumnus (A13) stated about the "tap into yourself" assignment, "The entire process was transformational, even when I didn't intend that or want that." Some of the doctoral programs are heavier in their usage of reflective assignments than others. Alumni from each of the four schools reported personal growth due to self-reflection.

Likewise, some of the doctoral programs are heavier than others in the usage of practical assignments. Practicum experiences were not overtly assigned in all of the programs. However, in spite of this, many of the alumni reported that they had experienced contexts in which they were able to apply knowledge gained through their doctoral studies. Direct application of theory from the classroom to the work environment was specifically mentioned by alumni (from each of the four schools) as a factor that influenced their learning and development.

Only brief comments were made by the faculty about the dissertation such as "The final assessment as to whether students have been successful in learning is the completion of a rigorous dissertation to the standards of the committee" (F4). Alumni spoke in reference to their dissertations only from the standpoint of enjoying their topic or the increased strength they gained through the rigorous process.

THE CONTRIBUTION OF ALUMNI

One would presume that in a professional research doctoral degree, graduates would be expected to both contribute to the knowledge of the field and be effective practitioners. The expectation that alumni would contribute through publications and strong professional practice makes sense with the broad aims of a professional research doctorate, according to Gardner (2009c). Faculty interviews highlighted six indicators of successful alumni: (a) postgraduate publications, (b) contributing to the profession, (c) a strong professional performance, (d) an ability to critically reflect, (e) a learning posture, and (f) helping others to learn. Alumni interviews highlighted three significant contributions that they collectively have made to the field: publications, effective practice, and developing the next generation of leaders.

Given the fact that faculty members were asked to provide names of alumni who exhibit the indicators of successful graduates, it is not surprising that the alumni actually embody those characteristics. Looking at the alumni findings in an aggregate form, all of the indicators of success named by the faculty were demonstrated. However, upon closer inspection, there is quite a bit of diversity of contribution among the individuals.

Postgraduate publication was an expected indicator of success for both faculty and alumni. If an alumnus had published after his or her doctorate degree had been completed, it was usually the first thing he or she mentioned when asked about the "most significant contributions to the field." Likewise, if the alumnus had not published postgraduation, some sort of admission was made as to the lack of publication and why that was the case. Clearly the expectation is that professional research doctoral graduates are expected to publish after they complete their degrees.

Strong professional performance in one's organization was an expected indicator of success for both faculty and alumni. Several graduates mentioned developing their home-base organizations as a significant contribution. The idea of being a scholar-practitioner or practitioner-scholar has also penetrated the identity of at least some of the alumni in that they mentioned the dual roles that they carry. For example, more than half of the alumni mentioned being an adjunct faculty either in their interviews or on their CVs or résumés.

Another indicator of success mentioned by faculty was being a lifelong learner and helping others to learn. Several alumni named developing the next generation of leaders as a "most significant contribution to the field." When alumni spoke about this contribution, several of them made statements about how this was important work and very meaningful to them as individuals.

The aggregate form of alumni demonstrated the indicators of success named by faculty. It would be fair to say that a continuum exists among alumni as to the actual expression of these indicators on an individual level much like the "scholar-practitioner continuum" described in the literature (Wasserman & Kram, 2009).

NOTES

1. Each of the four learning outcomes was mentioned by at least one or more faculty members from each school.

2. The learning outcomes from Chapter 4, which include contribution to the field, alumni as agents of change, and alumni as scholar practitioners, seemed to fit more naturally in the third section below that addresses "Contributions," so they will be addressed there.

3. Growth in confidence as a learning outcome was specifically mentioned by only one faculty member, and it was in relation to having confidence in research abilities rather than a more broad, sweeping self-confidence.

4. The study by Harris (2007) also found that building relationships with cohort members in doctoral education was important for the students.

PART III

IMPLICATIONS OF THE RESEARCH

Part I looked at some of the precedent literature that informs this research, and the findings of the study were reported in Part II. The third part of this volume will look at the implications of this research for the fields of OD and doctoral education. Chapters 8 and 9 will begin to address two literature gaps that were mentioned in the introduction. Chapter 8 will delve into the first literature gap of the development of the OD professional. The ninth chapter will explore the gap in research surrounding the development of doctoral students. Chapter 10 will close out this work by articulating some observations about the tensions that are inherent in doctoral education.

CHAPTER 8

DEVELOPING OD PRACTITIONERS

The precedent literature delineates the competencies needed to be an effective OD practitioner (Cummings & Worley, 2009; Kahnweiler, 2006; Worley & Feyerherm, 2003). Understanding the necessary competencies for practice is important; however, a gap in the research exists in how OD professionals are developed (Kahnweiler, 2006). An argument could be made that pursuing a doctoral degree is an extreme form of professional development (Boud & Lee, 2009; Jebril, 2008). With that in mind, it is significant that the context of this study was four professional research doctoral programs that attract midcareer working professionals. The alumni who were chosen for this study are successful professionals who share a desire to learn and grow throughout their lifetime. All of them have some affiliation with the field of OD, and all but one of the alumni interviewed have management experience. The feedback that the alumni in this study gave with regard to what helped them to learn throughout their doctoral degree can be useful in addressing how to develop OD professionals outside of a higher-education format. Obviously not everything from an academic setting is transferable to a nonacademic setting, yet much can be gleaned that gives food for thought about developing OD practitioners. Since a significant gap exists in the literature on this topic, any research that provides knowledge in this arena should prove to be helpful. The factors that the alumni of these programs mentioned that influenced their learning and development as professionals will hopefully shed light on the issue of how to develop OD practitioners. Several of these factors are described below.

Educating the Scholar Practitioner in Organization Development, pp. 119–125
Copyright © 2012 by Information Age Publishing
All rights of reproduction in any form reserved.

CRITICAL REFLECTION

The theme of intense critical reflection emerged as an important element of personal and professional development for alumni. Faculty members named the ability to critically reflect as an indicator of success. Mezirow (1991) believes critical reflection is the process of "assessing the content, process, or premise(s) of our efforts to interpret and give meaning to an experience" (p. 104). Critical reflection may be used to assess many different aspects of self and profession. For example, critical reflection on one's own taken-for-granted assumptions regarding using theory to inform practice is important. Constraining or obsolete assumptions about the ways that theory can or cannot inform practice might hold a person back in their development as an OD professional. Another example would be to critically reflect from another person's vantage point; this is essential for an OD practitioner in order to broaden one's own perspectives and build empathy and understanding for the other person's view. Both of these examples illustrate being a "reflective practitioner" or one who has the capability to reflect-in-action (Schön, 1983, 1987). Additionally, the skill of learning to mentor or coach others in the art of reflection is another potential area of growth for the OD professional.

SELF-KNOWLEDGE

Another particular type of critical reflection is aimed at the self in terms of growth in emotional and social intelligence. Stated in a different way, for the OD practitioner, "intrapersonal" knowledge is crucial (Cummings & Worley, 2009, p. 53). Several faculty members from this study mentioned self-development as an important learning outcome for students of OD. Understanding and knowing one's self is essential for the OD professional, since the work of OD is highly relational, especially with regard to building mutual respect and trust with a client or coworker.

Alumni underscored "the use of self as instrument" as a reason that OD practitioners should be critically reflective about themselves. Knowledge of self includes challenging constraining tacit assumptions about one's personal or professional view of self. Once the assumptions are challenged, then the person has the opportunity to discover a more authentic view of self that will have the potential to guide future courses of action. The assignments given by faculty that "provoke" reflection are a way of encouraging the practitioner to challenge existing assumptions about self. Faculty member (F13) described an assignment given in class to promote reflection,

I provoke as a first major assignment a personal vision statement. I want them to look at their core values. I want them to look at their operating philosophy. I want them to look at their fantasies. I want them to look at their passion, there sense of legacy, their calling. I want them to contemplate their noble purpose in life. I want them to think about their intellectual agenda. And then I push them into even considering their family relationships, their intimate relationships with their spouse or partner, or finding one if they don't have one. I want them contemplate their spiritual health, their physical health, their contributions to community.

The reflective assignments given by faculty spurred self-reflection in several of the alumni. For example, alumnus (A13) stated,

The instructors had always talked about self-as-instrument: that you really have to tap into yourself, and you really have to understand yourself, be self-aware before you can really work with anybody else. And I thought, "Oh, yeah, blah, blah, blah." But I realized as part of this one class, that it was really at the core of everything; and so that was a total awakening for me, and the turning on its ear of something that I had held true for thirty years working. In my professional background, it was all about the client ... what I thought or how I felt or how I approached things really didn't matter. So that was super exciting; to come from one position and hold it so stridently and then, through the process of working with others, of learning—of learning about myself, and learning about learning—I changed. The entire process was transformational; even when I didn't intend that or want that.

The previous quote highlighted the upending of assumptions that this person held on to for many years. Transformation around the idea of "self-as-instrument" was not intended or wanted, and yet it happened. Other alumni spoke about inner change that happened as a result of their own pursuit of it. Participant (A3) stated,

The program is very adamant about developing reflective practitioners; and I wouldn't say we were forced necessarily, but each of the courses involved a significant component around personal reflection. By taking advantage of that, it was a huge growth opportunity and really life transforming.... And the opportunity to make time for personal reflection really provided me insights into what makes me tick and how I work with others.

Each of these professionals learned more about themselves as a result of their reflective experiences. Alumnus (A20) gave an example of a specific assignment that provided the opportunity for growth in self-knowledge. Participant (A20) stated,

I have always known on the surface what my values were, but this required us to write them down and to really think about what are the core values that we walk around with. That's something that the whole program required: a lot of reflection. But this one course required it in a more personal level, and I found that really rewarding. I mean, I have always had a kind of personal reflective quality, but this was one where I guess I had never really taken the time to look specifically at some of the things they asked us to look at within myself. That really helped to hone my understanding of who I am, what I believe in, and what is important to me, and that has helped me to frame what I want to do in my consulting business moving forward.

Surfacing and attempting to understand the tacit assumptions about one's self and one's career is what is in view here. The self-knowledge gained in the process allowed this person to think ahead about the next season of their life armed with a better understanding of self. The hard work of self-reflection is not necessarily an academic exercise. It takes significant amounts of time, and it takes discipline, but, as illustrated in the above quotes from alumni, the fruits of self-reflection are worth the effort.

PROFESSIONAL IDENTITY AND SOCIALIZATION

For the OD practitioner, growth in professional identity is an appropriate developmental task. Professional identity is defined as a "constellation of attributes, beliefs, values, motives, and experiences in terms of which people define themselves in a professional role"; it aligns with one's personal identity development and is relatively stable over time (Ibarra, 1999, p. 764). Aligning vocational choices with one's personal identity is necessary so that an inner dissonance is not created between one's personal identity and one's professional identity. Critical reflection on one's authentic and individuated self and one's vocation is foundational to professional development (Cranton & King, 2003).

Authentic self-knowledge, feedback from other professionals, varied experiences in the workplace, and growth in professional status all build professional identity (Jebril, 2008). Components of professional status include "a set of philosophical assumptions, a specific body of knowledge, a code of ethics, a domain of concern, aspects of practice" and "the use of legitimate tools" (pp. 2, 35). These components of building professional status can be used to encourage the development of professional identity in OD practitioners.

For the OD practitioner, as well as other types of practitioners, professional identity is "culturally ascribed" (Jebril, 2008, p. 36). In other words, socialization into the OD field helps the OD practitioner to form professional identity. The process of socialization encourages a person to internalize characteristics, values, attributes, and knowledge of their profession, and develop skills that contribute to a growing professional self (O'Meara, 2008). In this current study, socialization into the field was an important factor that was mentioned by faculty and alumni. Providing a connection to the broader field through mentoring, meeting with a cohort or a professional network group, exposure to thought leaders or leading practitioners, and attendance and participation in professional and academic conferences seem to be an important means of development of professional identity as well as socialization into the field.

LEARNING STIMULATED THROUGH NEW INPUT

Many adult educators endorse self-directed learning as an effective mode of learning for adults (Brookfield, 1990; Knowles, 1988; Vella, 1994). Planning and managing one's own learning is appropriate for OD professionals. For example, one factor that influenced doctoral graduates' learning and development was being immersed in theory that had a direct application toward practice. Alumni spoke about the classroom discussions that were immediately transferable to their work environments as being a time they were "most excited about learning." Others mentioned doing research to build links of theory with practice (and practice with theory) as significant learning experiences.

In the broader OD practitioner population, making theory and practice linkages may also stimulate learning and professional growth. However, there are other ways of being stimulated by new input rather than focusing on theory and subject-matter content. Varying one's work experiences to include more international work or volunteering one's time and expertise to a nonprofit organization are sources of fresh input that will challenge the growth of the OD practitioner. Another source of input would be to seek out leaders in the field through attending professional or academic conferences. Alumni spoke of being encouraged and inspired by these industry and thought leaders. Finally, the challenge to be a steward of the discipline by making a contribution through creation of knowledge and improving practice is another tangible way of challenging the ongoing development of the OD professional. According to faculty members and alumni, being a lifelong learner and sharing what one learns is an indicator of a successful professional.

SOCIAL LEARNING AND COLLABORATION

Alumni overwhelmingly point to their cohort experiences as a factor that contributed to their learning and development. The broader implication could be that OD professionals like learning in a social or collaborative manner. The cohort provided cultural diversity and a variety of industry experience that were stimulating to those involved. Dialogue and debate around theory and practice were stimulating to the alumni in this study, and they enjoyed building professional relationships with their cohort members. Consequently, providing learning opportunities that are social in nature rather than providing isolated individualized learning opportunities seems to be significant to OD professionals.

One avenue through which OD practitioners can pursue social learning is collaboration with other practitioners or academics. Collaborating on a research or work project brings fresh perspectives to the table, causes each of the collaborators to be challenged, and hopefully will benefit the project. The theory-practice gap is more likely to be bridged when researchers and practitioners work together on business or organizational challenges.

Another means of social learning is through networking and mentoring. Alumni mentioned both of these avenues of learning as important to their professional growth. Intentionally seeking out networking opportunities at conferences or other professional gatherings can be mutually beneficial to both parties. Deliberately pursuing mentoring opportunities is also a great way to stimulate one's professional growth.

A "mentoring constellation" of opportunities provides the individual with different types of challenges and encouragement (Stanley & Clinton, 1992). Seeking out someone who is more experienced or has a skillset that you desire to learn from is the traditional way of thinking about mentoring. However, in terms of a mentoring constellation, there are many other types of opportunities that exist. For example, being a peer mentor with a colleague inside your organization has the benefit of helping one another to understand the corporate culture and doubles the potential network of opportunities available. Being a peer mentor with a colleague outside your organization affords the opportunity to be more vulnerable with your own growth goals and provides a potential means of accountability. Internal peer mentors have the potential to be "allies," whereas external peer mentors have the potential to be "confidants" (Heifetz, Grashow, & Linsky, 2009). Being a traditional "downward mentor" to an inexperienced colleague provides a fresh stream of curiosity to challenge tacit assumptions about your practice that may be obsolete (Stanley & Clinton, 1992). In addition, if the person you are mentoring is significantly younger, they can provide great insight into the current thinking of that generation, if they are encouraged to do so.

A final point of application with regard to social learning is becoming skilled in the art of dialogue. The word dialogue literally means "flow of meaning" and thus a dialogical conversation is one in which shared meaning is built (Bohm, 1996). The competencies of dialogue are listening, respecting, voicing, and suspending (Isaacs, 1999). Growing in the skills and attitudes of dialogue promotes generative inquiry, greater collaboration, and effective practice (Colwill, 2005).

In summary, some of the ways doctoral students are developed in their educational programs could be applied to the broader professional development of OD practitioners, since these doctoral programs attract midcareer professionals, and it was these professionals who spoke about the factors that influenced their development. A few of these developmental processes are

- critical reflection regarding one's professional role and practice;
- intense reflection toward self-knowledge and personal development;
- demonstrating and coaching others in how to be a reflective practitioner;
- actively building one's professional identity;
- socialization into the field through mentoring, meeting with a cohort or a professional work group, exposure to thought leaders or leading practitioners, and attendance and participation in professional and academic conferences;
- acquiring the skills to be a self-directed learner;
- purposefully engaging one's self with new stimulating input;
- becoming a "steward of the discipline" by generating new knowledge, improving practice, and sharing knowledge with others in the field;
- discussing and debating OD theory with a view toward practice;
- directly applying theory in practice;
- engaging in learning opportunities that are social or collaborative in nature;
- pursuing a mentoring constellation with a variety of relationships; and
- learning the attitudes and skills of genuine dialogue.

In the same way that doctoral students exhibit sacrifice and determination to complete their degree, the OD practitioner as a lifelong learner must actively and intentionally follow through on managing their own professional development. Learning and change usually require sacrifice, but as many of the alumni stated, they were so glad that they made that investment in themselves.

CHAPTER 9

DEVELOPING SCHOLAR-PRACTITIONER DOCTORAL STUDENTS

As stated above, research on doctoral education has increasingly grown over the past decade (Lee & Boud, 2009; Nerad, 2008). Despite the increase in research, the developmental needs of the doctoral student have not yet been thoroughly examined (Gardner, 2009b). In particular, what is "lacking is any serious effort to engage many of those former students in the conversation about how to improve doctoral education" (C. Taylor, 2009, p. 54). Listening to alumni discuss their educational experiences is of prime importance, and according to Taylor (2009), it is not being done effectively. This gap in the literature was one of the motivations for this current study. Chapter 9 focuses on some ideas from this research that could potentially help doctoral faculty and administrators in the development of their students.

SOLICIT FEEDBACK FROM THE ALUMNI

If the doctoral student is truly the focus of the educational process, and if educators desire to improve their practice, then it makes sense to listen to the insights of alumni regarding their educational experiences. A good practice for any doctoral program would be to conduct a qualitative study with their recent graduates in order to gain the perspectives of alumni about their educational experience.

Educating the Scholar Practitioner in Organization Development, pp. 127–134
Copyright © 2012 by Information Age Publishing
All rights of reproduction in any form reserved.

In setting up the research design for this project, the approach could have been to ask alumni to identify the problems of doctoral education with the overall intention of trying to fix these issues. However, this was not the orientation of this research project. This research has been approached in an appreciative manner, meaning the researcher wanted to find out what is working well in doctoral education with the hope that these elements could be built upon. As a result, the aggregate of findings from the four schools and from the perspectives of both the faculty and alumni provide a clear picture of what is working well. The alumni named six factors that influenced their learning and professional development: (a) research experience, (b) engaging in new professional opportunities, (c) encouraging direct application of theory, (d) being mentored, (e) exposure and networking with leaders of the field, and (f) the richness of the cohort experience (Colwill, 2011). Exploring each of these factors could be a next step for administrators and faculty of the schools that participated in this study as they seek to build on what is already working well.

INTEGRATION OF MULTIPLE IDENTITIES

An interesting observation that was highlighted in this research was the unique student population of the doctoral programs that participated in the study. This section focuses on one of the pressing needs of the professional research doctoral students: integration of multiple identities.

Professional research doctoral programs tend to attract midcareer practitioners as students. On the one hand, having a student population that is rich with valuable experience makes the dialogue and debate around substantive topics very interesting. On the other hand, the formation of their professional identities at midcareer may be well-developed, and putting students within a context where they are being asked to integrate a "scholar identity" alongside their practitioner identity can be very difficult for some people.

Professional identity is relatively stable, consequently when doctoral students are asked to stretch themselves to incorporate new behaviors, values, and ways of seeing themselves, it can cause stress. The observation has been made that "most doctoral students face disjunctures between their sense of self as an adult, their placement as a novice in an expert scholar community, and their development of this new identity as a scholar and knowledge creator" (Kasworm & Bowles, 2010, p. 225). When two identities are vying for attention, there will be stress to the point of being a "disorienting dilemma" (Mezirow, 1991). As a result, a negative effect on professional identity may happen through "professional role ambiguity, role erosion, role extension, and unclear definition for a profession" (Jebril, 2008, p. 36).

Students who get stuck in a disorienting dilemma may need guidance from the faculty. For the faculty to provide help, an awareness of the literature on professional identity, professional development, and transformative learning may be in order.[1] Acting on this knowledge may have a positive effect on the individual student's development as a professional, as well as aiding the intentional socialization process of the student into the field. In essence, cooperation and encouragement with these developmental processes could provide greater support and more opportunity to learn for the doctoral student.

If the faculty can help students learn the art of critical reflection, developing new ways of interpreting their experiences and providing guidance in the movement toward a more authentic expression of themselves, then the multiple identity tension may be eased for the student. Since professional identity and personal identity are closely related, the scholar-practitioner dissonance that is awakened in the student during doctoral studies will hopefully come to a point of resonance. Thus, developing self-knowledge through critical reflection and effective feedback from others is crucial for the scholar-practitioner doctoral student.

One very tangible way faculty can help students integrate their multiple identities is to share their own strategies and stories of how they went through this process themselves. Recent alumni could also be asked to share their experiences of how they critically reflected on their experiences and made new meaning out of the disorientation. In addition, introducing doctoral students to an abbreviated form of transformative learning theory may lessen the anxiety somewhat since students will realize that what they are experiencing is actually part of the developmental process of becoming a scholar-practitioner.

UNIQUE SOCIALIZATION PROCESSES

One of the interesting concepts that surfaced out of this research is that the schools that were involved have distinct cultures and different ways of socializing their students into the field of OD. Some schools placed heavy emphasis on research capabilities; some schools highlighted the practical skillsets of the OD profession; some schools required substantial amounts of reflection; and some schools promoted involvement in academic conferences and publishing. None of the schools placed heavy emphasis on all of these elements. What each program highlighted as important or valuable seemed to be the primary means of socialization. For example, if faculty members believe that attending and presenting at academic conferences is a superb means of socialization into the field, and if they model it for the students and nudge students into the experience, then the students who follow through on the experience of participating at conferences are explicitly or implicitly rewarded with professional status as a scholar-practitioner. This professional status has a socializing effect on the student.

The faculty and alumni spoke about the types of socialization that happened in each of the four doctoral programs. A few of the socializing activities that alumni mentioned in this study were being provided with new professional opportunities, being mentored, exposure to thought leaders and leading practitioners, cowriting with a professor, being a paper reviewer for conference papers or a journal, serving as a leader or board member of a professional or academic association, networking with leaders in the field, overseas consulting opportunities, and working on projects with one's cohort that contribute to the field. Again, none of the schools emphasized all of these. However, the broader point for faculty and administrators is to be fully aware of how and toward what they are attempting to socialize their students and knowing whether or not their espoused socialization really lines up with their actual socialization values, processes, and activities.

SCHOLAR-PRACTITIONER DEVELOPMENT

As mentioned above, the unique student population that the professional research doctorate attracts poses both significant strengths and distinct challenges. The focus of this section is on some of the specific elements of development that were named by the faculty and the alumni that made an impact on student's learning with regard to scholar-practitioner identity formation.

Individual Attention

One of the elements that faculty members mentioned in the interviews with regard to creating a learning environment was providing students with individual attention. For example, faculty member (F18) maintained that

> These are students who have careers, they have backgrounds; it became clear probably in the second or third year of my teaching that what we were really doing was we were helping to shape and mold people in the directions that they desired but on a path that we could call OD. The individual student came in unique and left unique. But there was an affinity for a core set of values that underpin our field. But how a person approaches that

work, it became more and more clear to me, was very individualistic, and this has been true particularly in our last couple of classes.

The tension between fostering the student's unique identity and the socialization into the field is expressed in the above quote. In Chapter 6, alumni mentioned several ways that the individual attention that they received from faculty made an impact upon them. In most cases, the individualized attention provided opportunities for professional development. Cranton (2006) names three essential components of professional development: individuation, authenticity, and transformative learning. The individual attention given by faculty appears to have helped with all three of these components of professional development for doctoral students. The influence of faculty upon students appears to be strong. What follows below are some of the developmental experiences that faculty and alumni spoke about in their interviews that made a learning impact.

Navigating the Scholar-Practitioner Challenge

One of the tensions that students need to sort out is the multiple identity challenge of being a scholar-practitioner while in the doctoral program. Some of the alumni in the research study embraced the new identity of scholar-practitioner and carried it on postgraduation; others stepped more fully into the practitioner identity; a few shifted toward the scholar identity and became full-time tenure-track faculty. The developmental experiences that faculty provided to socialize students into becoming a steward of the discipline were varied. The individualized attention given to students provided challenges in the areas that they had the least experienced in and also where they had their greatest strengths. Alumni mentioned that they benefitted from many different professional opportunities that were opened up by the faculty and the networking provided through being in the doctoral program. Some of these experiences include

- reflective assignments on self-assessment and personal vision;
- specific mentoring by faculty regarding the developmental needs of the student (i.e., in the arena of social or emotional intelligence);
- mentoring on professional developmental challenges;
- allowing students to facilitate discussions and co-consult with professors in implementing Appreciative Inquiry Summits or World Café experiences;
- providing opportunities for students to write chapters in books;

- opening doors for students to be board members of organizations;
- nominating students to hold leadership positions within professional associations;
- copresenting at a conference with a professor or seasoned practitioner;
- cowriting an article or paper with a faculty member;
- exposure and networking with thought leaders and leading practitioners;
- encouraging students to write their own papers/presentations for submission to conferences;
- challenging students to collaborate on work projects or academic conference submissions together with other cohort members;
- varied practicum experiences, including overseas work;
- consulting opportunities;
- leading a discussion during classtime or on the Internet with other cohort members;
- teaching a class at the master's level;
- making presentations on their current research to newly formed cohorts; and
- encouraging students to pursue being adjunct faculty members.

These are several of the ways the faculty and the broader community of OD encouraged the development of the alumni in this study. In addition to what is stated above, Chapter 8 lists developmental experiences for the education of the practitioner of OD.

The research of Ibarra (1999) has shown that diverse experiences and meaningful feedback from colleagues help people gain insight about themselves and their specific professional preferences. For the alumni, trying on these different experiences and receiving feedback helped them to discover their authentic strengths and step more fully into them.

IMPORTANCE OF THE COHORT MODEL

The cohort experience seemed to be a highlight for many of the alumni in this study. Deliberately building on the cohort experience could provide even greater learning impact. One wonders if it is possible to be even more deliberate in the use of the cohort model of education at the doctoral level. What other ways might the cohort model be used more intentionally to socialize the individual members into the field? In what ways could the cohort be the platform for students to explore the integration of the multiple identities they are juggling during their doctoral studies? Could the cohort model be used to help develop or hone professional collaboration skills within the group?

Many questions could be raised with regard to building on the learning experiences within the cohort. One question of particular importance that was raised from alumni interviews is "Could termination of the official cohort experience be more deliberately channeled toward learning?" This question is pertinent since several alumni expressed a deeply felt loss over leaving behind the comfort of the official cohort meetings to write their dissertations in isolation; termination was a significant distraction for some and proved to be an obstacle for others. Perhaps this sense of loss could be mitigated by viewing it as an opportunity for development and deliberately discussing the impending small-group termination process during the last full year of meetings. An honest discussion about what the group desires to be an appropriate closure may help ease the transition and provide a strategy and more support for people to successfully complete the dissertation phase of the process.

FOCUSING ON LEARNING OUTCOMES

The last element that could prove helpful for faculty and administrators of doctoral programs is to focus even more intently on learning outcomes for their students. Being clear about learning outcomes at the teaching-level event, the course level, and the program level will help students navigate the stressful waters of doctoral education a little easier. Introducing other creative and effective ways of thinking about learning outcomes may prove to be helpful (Fink, 2003). Perhaps designing learning outcomes around aspects of professional identity formation might be of benefit; for example, the components that build professional status: "a set of philosophical assumptions, a systematic body of knowledge, a code of ethics, a domain of concern, aspects of practice" (Jebril, 2008, p. 35) and the use of "legitimate tools" (p. 2). Another avenue of potential pursuit would be to design learning outcomes around being a steward of the discipline (i.e., creating, conserving, and transforming knowledge).

In addition, paying more attention to the positive hidden curriculum of the coursework and degree program is a small factor that could potentially have a sizable effect. For instance, the finding that doctoral-education instilled discipline and commitment through the rigors of research seems to be an unintended learning outcome. Recognizing this finding, faculty could be more deliberate in providing appropriate challenge and support that will help in the development of discipline and commitment.

Unearthing some of the tacit learning outcomes of one's doctoral program may prove to be helpful for both faculty and students alike.

Broadly speaking, the goal of doctoral education is to foster learning and development of individuals who will become the stewards of the discipline. Observations from this study that might help faculty members and administrators in the education of scholar practitioner doctoral students included

- soliciting feedback from alumni about their educational experience through a qualitative study;
- intentionally preparing faculty to help students find their way through the multiple identity crisis that may occur in their doctoral studies;
- understanding, articulating, and building on the unique socialization values, processes, and activities of the individual program;
- providing direct individual attention, support, and challenge to students in their development as scholar-practitioner professionals;
- more intentional and deliberate use of the cohort model of education in fostering learning for students; and
- stepping more fully into the use of creative and effective learning outcomes.

Chapters 8 and 9 have looked at the ways in which this research could inform two of the current literature gaps that were described in the introduction of this work. The next chapter will provide a reflective angle of observation regarding the practice of doctoral education.

NOTE

1. Several of the faculty members in this study are versed in transformative learning theory.

CHAPTER 10

TOWARD A
CULTURE OF LEARNING

In drawing this work to a conclusion, I will shift to first-person narration to share some of my observations and reflections. In approaching this topic, I have an unusual perspective: I am a professor who teaches doctorate courses; in the recent past, I have worked as a consultant and leader, and I have also recently completed a second PhD degree. As a result of my varied background, I have a sincere appreciation for the experience bases of both the alumni and the faculty in this study. However, the pursuit of the second doctorate afforded me a vantage point in which I was naturally making comparisons between my first and second degrees. Something I noticed early during the second doctorate experience was that each of my graduate programs had unique sets of strengths as well as distinctive "cultures of learning."[1] Through the second doctorate, I have gained knowledge in a new field of study, but I also have grown personally and professionally in new and different ways as a result of participating in the second educational experience. I began to wonder if the differences that I was noticing were due to the fact that these programs are in different disciplines of study, or if each doctoral program (no matter what the discipline) simply has its own distinctive culture.[2]

Although faculty members are responsible for using the best resources possible to create a stimulating learning environment for students, I have observed that both faculty members and students participate in creating a culture of learning at the doctoral level of study. In addition, the co-creation of learning may be more pronounced in a cohort model of education (than

Educating the Scholar Practitioner in Organization Development, pp. 135–141

other modes of education) due to the egalitarian collaborative philosophy that supports its premise.

Collegial doctoral work lends itself to several inherent tensions. Both faculty and students influence these tensions, and the ways in which faculty and students manage them helps to create a distinct learning culture. The remainder of this work focuses on several of these tensions that I have observed from my own experience and from listening to the experiences of faculty and alumni within this research project.

Theory and Practice

Some people are more comfortable with concepts and theory, while others prefer a concrete, pragmatic view of the world. When these different types of individuals are grouped together and begin to discuss OD topics, the theory-practice tension quickly surfaces. In the interviews with alumni, many of the graduates labeled themselves with regard to where they felt most comfortable with regard to this tension. Some were on the theoretical side, others were on the practical side, and still others liked having a foot in both camps.

As doctoral faculty and students seek to manage this theory-practice tension, it shapes how learning takes place, and it contributes to the professional identity development of the people involved. How are the practitioner-oriented individuals encouraged to embrace the notion of being a scholar and steward of the discipline? How are the more theoretical individuals challenged to concretely apply their learning? How do those who operate in dual roles navigate their multiple professional identities successfully? Developing harmony within this tension can potentially foster a better understanding of both theory and practice, as well as help develop the professional identity of students and faculty as scholar-practitioners or practitioner-scholars.

Challenge and Support

Managing the tension of challenge and support is complicated. For instance, how proactive should a professor be in initiating additional challenges for students on top of the already rigorous doctoral program agenda? Should faculty members insert challenges into doctoral education that intentionally disequilibrate students in order to awaken a disorienting dilemma with the overall aim of transformative learning and professional or personal growth? It was my impression that several faculty members in this study require overseas assignments in their educational programs to expose students to other cultures, but also to deliberately create an experience ripe for disequilibration. In other words, professors intentionally use overseas experiences to provoke students to challenge their own taken-for-granted assumptions about all sorts of issues. A professor cannot cause transformative learning to happen, but he or she can set up an environment or conditions that make it more likely for this type of learning to occur. Knowing when and how to challenge a student requires wisdom and discernment. What are the boundaries for faculty in setting up learning environments that are likely to bring about this type of disorienting challenge?

On the other hand, what are the boundaries of supportive behavior on the part of faculty with students? Many alumni expressed gratitude for the support they received from the faculty through mentoring or through other avenues. However, if the faculty member offers help or support to the student, and it is unwanted by the student, it ceases to be helpful (Schein, 2009).

In addition, students face the tension of challenge and support with one another as peer teachers and peer learners in their cohorts. How do cohort members harmonize this tension within the group? Challenging one another or asking for and receiving support can be awkward and uncomfortable. However, the healthy navigation of this tension is important for the doctoral education experience. Both challenge and support are needed in the process (Gardner, 2009b).

Direct and Empower

Similar to the tension of challenge and support, I observed a tension between directing and empowering. In other words, how much or how little guidance and involvement should the faculty member give the student? The examples that were articulated in the alumni interviews illustrated more directive behavior on the part of faculty earlier in the degree program or when something particularly difficult was introduced to the students. On the flip side, alumni seemed to be more self-empowered later in the program to take charge of their own learning, culminating in the completion of their dissertation. It seems that the confidence the alumni gained in the process of participating in the degree program contributed to their own self-empowerment. In addition, as students took on more and more responsibility to participate in knowledge creation, greater empowerment was invested in them by faculty and other students.

Individual and Collaborative Learning

In a cohort model of education, each member is challenged to learn and perform on an individual basis as well as work and learn collaboratively with other participants. The tension of individual and collaborative learning seems to surface in group experiences. Many reasons probably exist for the bubbling up of this tension. One observation I have made as a professor is that when students are either very introverted in nature or they hold national cultural values that are highly individualistic, they may struggle more with the group work assignments. A quote by alumnus (A3) typifies this type of individualistic mindset:

> I went into the program in spite of the fact that it was cohort based. I didn't want to do anything to do with a cohort. I always saw myself as a lone wolf. Group projects were always a pain in the ###. Just let me do my thing and enjoy this and don't make me have to interact with a lot of other people. What I discovered was that the cohort was *extremely* important, and I developed lifelong friends.

This participant was outspoken in articulating this tension, yet eventually recognized the value of the relationships and collaboration that resulted in working with the other cohort members.

Other people experience stress from the tension of doing work that is individualized. The isolation of the dissertation process has been mentioned previously, and many students struggle with doing all of that work on their own. I believe managing the tension of individual and collaborative learning is important for professional growth and development.

Socialization and Individuation

Several faculty members made strong statements that one of the aims of doctoral education is to socialize students into the discipline. Faculty members exert pressure on students to socialize them into the field, and cohort members may exert peer pressure on one another to assimilate into the discipline as well. The tension for the doctoral student is between assimilating into the norms, values, practices, and rituals of the field and retaining an authentic individuation of professional self. Each doctoral student faces this pressure of integrating multiple identities (Kasworm & Bowles, 2010).

Teacher and Learner

The collegial nature of doctoral education blurs the categories of teacher and learner. The faculty are viewed as teachers, however as they support and empower students along the way, the co-creating of learning begins to happen more and more. Students gradually become peer teachers to the faculty and other students. As the phases of the education process unfold, it has been my observation that if this tension has been managed well, the dialogue that happens in the group is one of building shared meaning among peers. Healthy dialogue inspires generative inquiry, reflection and action (Bohm, 1996; Colwill, 2005; Freire, 1997; Isaacs, 1999). Managing the tension of being a peer teacher and a peer learner develops the self-directed learning muscles for being a lifelong learner and fosters the abilities to be a steward of the discipline in sharing knowledge with others.

Personal and Professional Growth

The alumni interviews pointed to many different types of growth that the participants experienced as a result of doctoral education. One of the interview questions for the alumni was, "In what ways did your doctoral education stretch you as a person and as a professional?" The question was phrased this way to allow people the freedom to speak about any type of growth that they experienced as a result of their education. Every alumnus interviewed made some type of comment about how they had been stretched or grown as an individual through participating in doctoral education. Some people kept distinct categories of personal and professional growth. Other people enmeshed the categories in favor of a more holistic way of viewing their growth. Several alumni spoke about the self-knowledge that they gained and the challenge of stepping into being a more authentic person in general. Examples were given of making changes in their professional world or career path that allowed for a more authentic fit. The shift toward a career that utilizes a more individuated genuine self is seen in the quote below:

> I think I am less excited about solving business performance problems of profitability or reducing costs, which used to excite me.... I recognize the importance, and so I don't think that I trivialize the business problems. I still like business problems, but I am less interested in those and more interested in ideas, personal vision, and growth in leadership because I think those could have the second-order impact on others and on the business as a consequent. I feel it has made me place a greater emphasis on human beings and human capital, and it fits well with my own philosophy of where I think I can make the most contributions. (A31)

Managing the tension of personal and profession growth through critical reflection fosters greater self-awareness and provides the opportunity to step into a position that is personally fulfilling and professionally challenging.

Sacrifice and Accomplishment

A tension exists between sacrifice and accomplishment for the doctoral student. The sacrifice shows up in the difficulty of the work, the amount of time that it takes to complete the degree, and the financial cost. It can also take a toll on family and friends:

> When you decide to do this, you live it. You live it not only when you show up at class, but you live it from what you take home, and your family lives it, and your friends live with it ... I am a high-off-the-charts "E" in Myers Brigg—an insane "E"—and so I had to tuck in all my edges, and I didn't see my friends as much and my spouse had to be very understanding ... from a personal standpoint, it is both challenging and requires that you become much more aware about what is important. (A10)

Managing time and priorities is one of the elements alumni mentioned as being important learning during the educational program. The delayed gratification of receiving the degree is only part of the accomplishment. The growth from the process can also be viewed as an accomplishment, much like completing a marathon is an accomplishment, so also is the strength that is gained in training for the race. I believe the tension of sacrifice and accomplishing is something many doctoral students face.

Endings and Beginnings

The tension of endings and beginnings is something both professors and students face numerous times in the course of doctoral work. Several alumni spoke about managing the transitions that happen during doctoral education. The transition of entering the doctoral program requires shifting one's life around to make room for being involved in the new educational adventure. Many other endings and beginnings happen for doctoral students as well: completing all of the coursework, drawing the official cohort experience to a close, finishing comprehensive exams, defending a dissertation proposal, conducting dissertation research, writing the dissertation document, defending the dissertation, and celebrating at graduation. Each of these transitions requires leaving behind what has become familiar and venturing into something new. Several alumni that doubted their ability to complete the doctoral program, after successfully finishing, wondered what other limitations they might be putting on themselves that were not warranted. The ending brought awareness of other possible new beginnings. Constraining assumptions were challenged and were overcome. Navigating the tension of endings and beginnings helps movement forward in one's life both personally and professionally.

The research study I conducted afforded me a great opportunity to learn from 54 prominent leaders in the field of organization development. I learned through the formal process of analyzing the data, reporting the findings, and discussing the implications, as well as through expressing my anecdotal thoughts and reflections about the tensions that need to be managed in the learning culture of a collegial doctoral environment. I am grateful to all of the participants who freely gave of their time in order to make this opportunity a reality.

NOTES

1. I am grateful to Dr. Peter Sorensen for naming this idea of a "culture of learning" for me. I do not know if he coined the phrase, but I first heard it from him.
2. The differences in the doctoral programs could be attributed to something entirely different as well.

APPENDIX 1

Research Methodology

The focus of this appendix is to give more detail on the research design and methodology used to conduct the study. This appendix consists of the following sections: research purpose and questions, rationale for the design, research participants, research methodology, and data analysis.

RESEARCH PURPOSE AND QUESTIONS

The overarching aim of this study was to investigate the impact of professional research doctoral programs on the learning and professional development of students who are all now graduates of their respective programs. The twofold purpose of this research was to look at the intended learning outcomes of four doctoral programs as reported by faculty and to explore the perceptions of doctoral alumni regarding their educational experience and how it contributed to their development as well as their current professional role. The research design was guided by specific research questions that emerged from the twofold purpose. The research questions prompting this study follows.

Faculty

1. What do doctoral faculty identify as the most important learning outcomes for their students, and what is the nature of these learning outcomes?

Educating the Scholar Practitioner in Organization Development, pp. 143–151
Copyright © 2012 by Information Age Publishing
All rights of reproduction in any form reserved.

2. How do doctoral faculty structure their programs to achieve these learning outcomes, and how are these learning outcomes assessed?

3. What do doctoral faculty identify as indicators of successful graduates of their programs, and what is the nature of these indicators of success?

Alumni

1. What do doctoral alumni identify as the most important learning that occurred while in their doctoral program?

2. Do alumni see any connection between their doctoral educational experience and their own professional development, and what is the nature, if any, of this connection?

3. What do doctoral alumni identify as their most important contributions to the field of OD or management?

RATIONALE FOR THE DESIGN

A qualitative approach was selected for this study. The reasons for this selection are threefold. The first reason is simply that the nature of the research questions dictated the methodological approach. The research questions required individualized conversations to allow both faculty and alumni to express their own views in their own words. Indeed, interviews provide the opportunity for the researcher to tap into "the inner experience of the participants" (Corbin & Strauss, 2008, p. 12). The second reason for a qualitative study was the need to lean more toward a "grounded theory"[1] type of study, since little is known about (a) the intentional development of OD professionals (Kahnweiler, 2006; Worley & Feyerherm, 2003), (b) the development of doctoral students (Gardner, 2009b; Kasworm & Bowles, 2010), and (c) the perspectives of doctoral graduates regarding their educational experience (Damrosch, 2009; C. Taylor, 2009). Interviews allow for the exploration of these topics in a manner that a quantitative approach could not have afforded. The third rationale for a qualitative approach was a pragmatic one. As stated above, graduate programs are not very good at keeping in touch with alumni (Damrosch, 2009). The pragmatic difficulty would have been in obtaining the contact information for a large enough bulk of the alumni from each school that could have supported a quantitative research approach. A qualitative study was workable with the sample size that was readily available.

RESEARCH PARTICIPANTS

The dissertation chair provided guidance in narrowing down which schools to include in the study. Four professional research doctoral programs featuring an emphasis or strong affiliation with the field of organization development were chosen to participate in this research project. Two of these are specifically identified as OD programs: one is a doctorate in education and the other a doctorate of philosophy. In order to broaden the sample, the remaining two programs are both doctorates of management with strong organization development underpinnings. All of these doctoral programs are listed in *The International Registry of Organization Development Professionals and Organization Development Handbook* (ODI, 2010).

The Four Doctoral Programs

The four professional research programs included in this study have commonalities and unique features. As stated above, all of the programs have an emphasis or a strong affiliation with the field of organization development. This affiliation with OD was the primary determinant of inclusion in the study. Another point of commonality among the programs is that they are housed in schools or universities that have home bases in the United States. Although the programs are all located in the United States, they are in different geographic regions.

Additional commonalities exist in the four programs. Each of the programs has a residency component in which on-the-ground, face-to-face gatherings with faculty and students occur on the home-base campus. Different formats occur for this residency component; some are a weekend format and others have intensive weeklong sessions. In addition to the residency component, three of the four programs have an element of online work (both collaborative and individual assignments) as part of their official coursework. Another commonality is that all of the programs have students participating in their programs who fly in from other regions of the United States and outside the United States.

A cohort model is employed in all of the programs in the study. The interpretation of that model is different depending on the culture of each program. However, broadly speaking, the common essence of the cohort model is that the students are formed into cohorts at the beginning of their educational journey, they attend classes together, at times work collaboratively together, learn from each other, and support each other throughout the process.

Each of these programs is a professional research doctorate, which implies other commonalities. The majority of students who are enrolled in these programs are full-time working professionals, most of whom are midcareer or late-career individuals. Many different types of full-time professions and industries are represented in the student populations. This type of midcareer student fits well with the ethos of the professional research doctorate, whose fundamental interest lies in developing scholar-practitioners or practitioner-scholars. As mentioned previously, professional research doctorate programs have an emphasis on rigorous research alongside of effective improvement of practice; all four programs share this philosophy. Three of the four campuses were visited by the researcher; time did not permit a visit to the fourth campus.

Faculty and Alumni Selection

The study was conducted with two populations: doctoral faculty and alumni.[2] At each school, the doctoral program director or a faculty member was contacted, asked to participate, and then asked for the names of other faculty members from their institution who might participate in the study. A total of 18 faculty members were interviewed from the four schools. The faculty members were invited to talk about what they believed to be the indicators of successful graduates. Once they named these indicators, they were asked to provide 8 to 10 names of alumni who embody these indicators of success. To be clear, alumni were selected through the recommendations of the faculty in the various schools participating in the study. The alumni contact information was obtained with the help of the program directors of each school. Graduates were asked to supply a current résumé or curriculum vitae. A total of 36 alumni were interviewed.

An element of participant bias may have been at work with the type of selection process used in this research. The faculty or program directors of each school chose alumni who embodied indicators of success to be participants in this study. However, they may have chosen not only successful alumni but also those individuals they knew would give a positive report about the program. Participant bias (not researcher bias) might have skewed the findings away from negative comments since the alumni participants were chosen by faculty or program directors.

The anonymity of the schools and the individual participants will be protected through delivering the findings of all four schools in an aggregate form. In reporting the findings in an aggregate form, the distinctive features of each program are absorbed into the whole. While it would have been interesting to put these schools side-by-side and make some comparisons, the decision was made to keep the findings in an aggregate form for several reasons. The first reason was to keep the anonymity of each school intact. The promise was made to each program representative that the findings would be reported in an aggregate form. Second, aggregate reporting increased the protection of each participant's privacy; it is much more difficult to identify one alumnus among 36 people and from four schools than it is to identify one alumnus among nine and from only one school. The last reason for keeping aggregate reporting was to focus the attention on doctoral education in the field of OD rather than allowing the findings to be used as a means of comparison or competition between schools.

Delimitations

The scope of the study was delimited to four professional research doctoral programs with emphasis or strong affiliation to the field of organization development. These parameters permitted a careful examination of the learning and professional development of students in these programs from the perspectives of both faculty and alumni.

Limitations

Since the research was delimited to faculty and alumni of four professional research doctorate programs with affiliations to the field of OD, the results of the research may be generalizable only with caution to (a) other types of doctoral programs, that is, research or professional doctorate programs; (b) disciplines outside the field of OD; and (c) professional research programs outside the United States.

RESEARCH METHODOLOGY

The research project was a qualitative study using in-depth interviews as the source of data. The interview protocol, included below, was developed from precedent literature and guided by the research questions. Pilot interviews with both faculty and alumni were conducted for the purpose of honing the interview questions. The participant selection process is described previously in the Faculty and Alumni Selection section. Participants were initially contacted in person, by phone, or by e-mail. They were given a brief explanation of the proposed research and asked to participate. Appointments for interviews of approximately 30 to 40 minutes

in duration were scheduled at the convenience of the research participants. Five of the interviews were conducted in person and the rest over
the phone. Permission was received from each of the participants to digitally record the interview.

Anonymity was protected by assigning a number to each faculty and
alumni participant. The anonymity of each school and each participant
was protected by reporting the findings in an aggregate form and by not
divulging any information that could potentially identify any of the individuals. Each participant was assigned a number. For example, faculty
members were randomly assigned F1, F2, F3, and so forth, and were
referred to by those numbers. The same holds true for alumni, although
their assigned numbers were A1, A2, A3, and so on.

In order to make the process more efficient, when the interviews from
one school were almost complete, the interviews for the next school were
set up and then conducted. This pattern was followed until the interviews
from all four schools were completed. The 54 interviews were conducted
during April, May, July, August, September, and October of 2010. Three
of the four schools were visited by the researcher during this time as well.

The interview process for the faculty and alumni included an opening
statement as to the broad purpose of the research study, asking for their
permission to record the interview, a few introductory questions, and then
the topical questions. Interviews were guided by the protocol below, but
questions were not always asked in the same order. Follow-up questions
were asked in response to the individual participant's responses. Interviews varied in length from 25 minutes to 60 minutes. If an interview time
approached the 25 minute mark, permission was asked to continue
beyond the agreed-upon appointment time of 30 minutes. The average
duration was approximately 30 minutes. The interviews were digitally
recorded, transcribed verbatim, and coded for generative themes.

Faculty Interview Protocol

After asking each participant's permission to record the interview,
some or all of the following introductory questions were asked to ease the
participant into the discussion:

- What courses do you teach?
- What do you enjoy the most about teaching doctoral students?
- What are the greatest strengths of your doctoral program?
- What are the unique features of your program?
- What are three wishes you have for your program?

Following the introductory questions, several topical questions, were asked of the faculty:

- What are you most hopeful that students will learn from being in this program?
- In addition to what you just mentioned, are there any other primary learning outcomes that you desire for students in this program?
- How do you teach to ensure that these learning outcomes are achieved?
- How do you assess these learning outcomes?
- What are the indicators of successful graduates of your program?
- Could you give me the names of alumni that you would like me to interview who embody these indicators of success that you mentioned?
- What advice would you give to new students entering into doctoral studies?
- We are at the end of the interview, is there anything else you would like to add that I have not asked you about, related to my topic?

At this point, each faculty member was thanked for his or her participation, and the names and contact information of the alumni were secured.

Alumni Interview Protocol

To start off the interview, the researcher made an initial comment about the participant's résumé or curriculum vitae to break the ice. After asking each participant's permission to record the interview, the following introductory questions were asked to ease the participant into the discussion:

- Please tell me about how you decided to pursue a doctorate degree.
- What did you expect to gain from the educational program when first entering?
- Were your expectations fulfilled?

Following the introductory questions, several topical questions were asked of each alumnus:

- Looking back at your doctoral education experience, could you tell me about a time when you were most excited about learning?

- In what ways did your doctoral education stretch you as a person and as a professional?
- How do you believe you have changed as a result of your doctoral education?
- What would you have changed about your educational experience if you could?
- Without being humble, what are the most significant contributions that you have made to the field of OD or management?
- What advice would you give to new students entering into doctoral studies?
- We are at the end of the interview, is there anything else you would like to add that I have not asked you about, related to my topic?

At this point each alumnus was thanked for his or her participation in the study.

The scope of the research was to reveal the personal perspectives of the alumni on their own growth, the courses, and the overall ethos of the educational program, but not regarding the administration, policies or logistical aspects of the program.

DATA ANALYSIS

Interviews were digitally recorded and transcribed verbatim. The transcriptions were printed in hard copy, coded, and analyzed by hand. Data analysis was performed in two rounds. The first round analyzed the transcriptions of alumni. The second round examined the transcriptions of faculty. Each round had three stages of analysis. In the first stage, the transcriptions were inductively analyzed by examining the texts of the interviews for similarities, dissimilarities, emerging themes, and theme exceptions. In the second stage of analysis, the texts were examined according to the research questions in which additional themes emerged. In other words, faculty responses were examined for learning outcomes, learning environment, and indicators of successful alumni. Similarly, alumni responses were reviewed for important learning, factors influencing learning and development, and contributions to the field. The third stage of analysis synthesized the themes of the first two stages into overall themes. Findings were delineated based on the overall themes that emerged from the data analysis.

NOTES

1. The term *grounded theory* is "a specific methodology developed by Glaser and Strauss (1967) for the purpose of building theory from data" (Corbin & Strauss, 2008, p. 1). This work uses the term in "a more generic sense to denote theoretical constructs derived from qualitative analysis" (p. 1).
2. Alumni were chosen to participate in the study instead of current students. The primary reason is that current students are still enmeshed in the educational process in which their outcome is not yet certain. They would not be able to fully evaluate their learning and the effect it has on their professional development since they have not yet completed the entire process.

APPENDIX 2

Further Research

Many avenues of research could be explored in following up on this study. A list of potential ideas for further research are named below:

- Diving deeper with the factors that influence development of students within the cohort experience;
- Investigating the role of peer teaching and learning in doctoral education;
- Looking at the specific impact of self-reflection assignments on professional development and socialization of doctoral students;
- Investigating the effects of practicum assignments; in particular, overseas practicum assignments;
- Exploring the identity shift from professional to researcher-as-professional as well as the strategies students use to make that transition smoother;
- Specifically exploring the transition phase of students when they end their classroom cohort experience and move to the dissertation phase;
- Unpacking the hidden curriculum of doctoral education as a theme of study;
- Looking more deeply at the assessments used in professional research doctoral education.

These are a few of the potential studies that could be investigated in extension of this current research study.

Educating the Scholar Practitioner in Organization Development, pp. 153–153
Copyright © 2012 by Information Age Publishing

REFERENCES

Anderson, T. (2001). The hidden curriculum in distance education. *Change, 33*(6), 28.

Armstrong, H. (2007). *Perceptions of value derived from an accelerated MBA program: A study of graduates and their managers*. Unpublished EdD, Teachers College, Columbia University, New York, NY.

Austin, A. E., & McDaniels, M. (2006). Using doctoral education to prepare faculty to work within Boyer's four domains of scholarship. *New Directions for Institutional Research, 2006*(129), 51–65.

Bohm, D. (1996). *On dialogue*. New York, NY: Routledge.

Boud, D., & Lee, A. (Eds.). (2009). *Changing practices of doctoral education*. New York, NY: Routledge.

Bourner, T. (1997). Teaching methods for learning outcomes. *Education & Training, 39*(9), 344–348.

Boyatzis, R., Cowen, S. S., & Kolb, D. A. (1995). *Innovation in professional education*. San Francisco, CA: Jossey-Bass.

Brookfield, S. D. (1990). *The skillful teacher*. San Francisco, CA: Jossey-Bass.

Brookfield, S. D. (2005). *The power of critical theory: Liberating adult learning and teaching*. San Francisco, CA: Jossey-Bass.

Brookfield, S. D., Kalliath, T., & Laiken, M. (2006). Exploring the connections between adult and management education. *Journal of Management Education, 30*(6), 828–839.

Brookfield, S. D., & Preskill, S. (1999). *Discussion as a way of teaching: Tools and techniques for democratic classrooms*. San Francisco, CA: Jossey-Bass.

Burke, W. W. (2006). Where did OD come from? In J. V. Gallos (Ed.), *Organization development: A Jossey-Bass reader* (pp. 13–38). San Francisco, CA: Jossey-Bass.

Chrite, E. L. (1998). *Knowledge, transfer and learning outcomes in university-based executive education*. Unpublished PhD, University of Michigan, Ann Arbor, MI.

Colbeck, C. L. (2008). Professional identity development theory and doctoral education. *New Directions for Teaching & Learning, 2008*(113), 9–16.

Colwill, D. (2005). *Dialogical learning and a renewed epistemology: Analysis of cultural and educational shifts from modernity toward postmodernity.* Deerfield, IL: Trinity International University.

Colwill, D. (2011). *Toward a culture of learning: The impact of professional research doctoral programs on graduates' learning and professional development.* Unpublished dissertation, Benedictine University, Lisle, IL.

Conger, J. A., & Xin, K. (2000). Executive education in the 21st century. *Journal of Management Education, 24*(1), 73–101.

Corbin, J., & Strauss, A. (2008). *Basics of qualitative research* (3rd ed.). Thousand Oaks, CA: SAGE.

Cranton, P. (2006). *Understanding and promoting transformative learning: A guide for educators of adults* (2nd ed.). San Francisco, CA: Jossey-Bass.

Cranton, P., & King, K. P. (2003). Transformative learning as a professional development goal. *New Directions for Adult & Continuing Education, 98,* 31.

Cummings, T. G., & Worley, C. G. (2009). *Organization development and change* (9th ed.). Mason, OH: South-Western Cengage Learning.

Damrosch, D. (2009). Vectors of change. In C. M. Golde & G. Walker (Eds.), *Envisioning the future of doctoral education* (pp. 34–45). San Francisco, CA: Jossey-Bass.

DeVeau, L. T. (1994). *Doctoral programs in hospitality administration: A Delphi study.* Unpublished EdD, University of Bridgeport, Bridgeport, CT.

Eidmann, B. C. (2002). *An analysis of educational leadership doctoral programs offered in California universities.* Unpublished EdD, University of La Verne, La Verne, CA.

Everson, S. T. (2009). A professional doctorate in educational leadership: St. Louis University's EdD program. *Peabody Journal of Education, 84*(1), 86–99.

Fink, L. D. (2003). *Creating significant learning experiences.* San Francisco, CA: Jossey-Bass.

Freire, P. (1997). *Pedagogy of the oppressed* (New Rev. 20th Anniv. ed.). New York, NY: Continuum.

Gardner, S. (2009a). Conceptualizing success in doctoral education: Perspectives of faculty in seven disciplines. *Review of Higher Education, 32*(3), 383–406.

Gardner, S. (2009b). The development of doctoral students: Phases of challenge and support. *ASHE Higher Education Report, 34*(6), 1–106.

Gardner, S. (2009c). Understanding doctoral education. *ASHE Higher Education Report, 34*(6), 29–40.

Gardner, S., & Mendoza, P. (2010). *On becoming a scholar: Socialization and development in doctoral education.* Sterling, VA: Stylus.

Garrett, R. U. (2006). *The quality of the doctoral experience in education at historically Black colleges and universities.* Unpublished PhD, University of North Texas, Denton, TX.

George, J. W. (2009). Classical curriculum design. *Arts & Humanities in Higher Education, 8*(2), 160–179.

Gibbons, M., Limoges, C., Nowotny, H., Schwartzman, S., Scott, P., & Trow, M. (1994). *The new production of knowledge: The dynamics of science and research in contemporary socities*. Thousand Oaks, CA: SAGE.

Gilbert, R. (2004). A framework for evaluating the doctoral curriculum. *Assessment & Evaluation in Higher Education, 29*(3), 299–309.

Gilbert, R. (2009). The doctorate as curriculum: A perspective on goals and outcomes of doctoral education. In D. Boud & A. Lee (Eds.), *Changing practice of doctoral education* (pp. 54–68). New York, NY: Routledge.

Gilbert, R., Balatti, J., Turner, P., & Whitehouse, H. (2004). The generic skills debate in research higher degrees. *Higher Education Research & Development, 23*(3), 375–388.

Golde, C. M. (2006). Preparing the steward of the discipline. In C. M. Golde & G. Walker (Eds.), *Envisioning the future of doctoral education* (pp. 3–20). San Francisco, CA: Jossey-Bass.

Golde, C. M. (2008). Applying lessons from professional education to the preparation of the professoriate. *New Directions for Teaching & Learning, 2008*(113), 17–25.

Golde, C. M., & Walker, G. (2006). *Envisioning the future of doctoral education*. San Francisco, CA: Jossey-Bass.

Green, B. (2009). Challenging perspectives, changing practices. In D. Boud & A. Lee (Eds.), *Changing practices of doctoral education* (pp. 239–248). New York, NY: Routledge.

Greene, K. (2007). *Alumni perceptions of the McNair scholars program at Kansas universities*. Unpublished PhD, Kansas State University, Manhattan, KS.

Harris, S. (2007). Critical reflections on doctoral learning. *Mentoring & Tutoring: Partnership in Learning, 15*(4), 331–332.

Hay, G. W. (2003). *The nature and significance of the executive doctoral scholar-practitioner of organizational development and change: A morphogenetic account of theory-practice linkages for the achievement of scholarly knowledge and business results.* Unpublished dissertation, Benedictine University, Chicago, IL.

Heifetz, R., Grashow, A., & Linsky, M. (2009). *The practice of adaptive leadership: Tools and tactics for changing your organization and the world*. Boston, MA: Harvard Business Press.

Hilgert, A. D. (1995). Developmental outcomes of an executive MBA programme. *Journal of Management Development, 14*(10), 64–76.

Horn, R. A. (2003). Developing a critical awareness of the hidden curriculum through media literacy. *Clearing House, 76*(6), 298–300.

Hubball, H., & Gold, N. (2007). The scholarship of curriculum practice and undergraduate program reform: Integrating theory into practice. *New Directions for Teaching & Learning*, (112), 5–14.

Huff, A. S., & Huff, J. O. (2001). Re-focusing the business school agenda. *British Journal of Management, 12*, S49–S54.

Hussey, T., & Smith, P. (2008). Learning outcomes: A conceptual analysis. *Teaching in Higher Education, 13*(1), 107–115.

Ibarra, H. (1999). Provisional selves: Experimenting with image and identity in professional adaptation. *Administrative Science Quarterly, 44*(4), 764–791.

Isaacs, W. N. (1999). *Dialogue and the art of thinking together.* New York, NY: Doubleday.

James, M., & Brown, S. (2005). Grasping the TLRP nettle: Preliminary analysis and some enduring issues surrounding the improvement of learning outcomes. *Curriculum Journal, 16*(1), 7–30.

Jebril, M. Y. (2008). *The evolution and measurement of professional identity.* Unpublished dissertation, Texas Woman's University, Denton, TX.

Kahnweiler, W. M. (2006). The development of OD careers: A preliminary framework for enacting what we preach. *Organization Development Journal, 24*(1), 10–21.

Kasworm, C., & Bowles, T. (2010). Doctoral students as adult learners. In S. Gardner & P. Mendoza (Eds.), *On becoming a scholar: Socialization and development in doctoral education* (pp. 223–241). Sterling, VA: Stylus.

Kelley, K. A. (2002). *Outcomes assessment of a Doctor of Pharmacy (Pharm.D.) program: Comparison of faculty and student perceptions of competency delivery and achievement.* Unpublished PhD, The Ohio State University, Columbus, Ohio.

Knowles, M. S. (1988). *The modern practice of adult education: From pedagogy to andragogy.* Englewood Cliffs, NJ: Cambridge Adult Education.

Kretovics, M. A. (1998). *Outcomes assessment: The impact of delivery methodologies and personality preference on student learning outcomes.* Unpublished PhD, Colorado State University, Fort Collins, CO.

Kretovics, M. A. (1999). Assessing the MBA: What do our students learn? *The Journal of Management, 18*(2), 125–136.

Lee, A., & Boud, D. (2009). Framing doctoral education as practice. In D. Boud & A. Lee (Eds.), *Changing practices of doctoral education* (pp. 10–25). New York, NY: Routledge.

Leisure, T. M. (2007). *Female graduate students' experiences in an online doctoral degree program: A heuristic inquiry.* Unpublished PhD, Capella University, Minneapolis, MN.

Mawhinney, J. (2009). *A determination of the essential outcomes for higher education supply chain management program success.* Unpublished EdD, Duquesne University, Pittsburgh, PA.

Mezirow, J. (1991). *Transformative dimensions of adult learning.* San Francisco, CA: Jossey-Bass.

Mezirow, J. (1996). Contemporary paradigms of learning. *Adult Education Quarterly, 46,* 158–172.

Mezirow, J. (2000). *Learning as transformation: Critical perspectives on a theory in progress.* San Francisco, CA: Jossey-Bass.

Nash, T. G. J. (2002). *Business curriculum development: A model for assessing outcomes in a university business curriculum using the Tyler Curriculum Model framework.* Unpublished EdD, Wayne State University, Detroit, MI.

Nerad, M. (2008). United States of America. In M. Nerad & M. Heggelund (Eds.), *Toward a global PhD? Forces and forms in doctoral education worldwide* (pp. 278–299). Seattle: University of Washington Press.

Nerad, M., & Heggelund, M. (Eds.). (2008). *Toward a global PhD? Forces and forms in doctoral education worldwide.* Seattle: University of Washington Press.

Nygaard, C., Holtham, C., & Courtney, N. (2009). Learning outcomes—politics, religion or improvement? In C. Nygaard, C. Holtham, & N. Courtney (Eds.), *Improving students' learning outcomes* (pp. 17–32). Portland, OR: Copenhagen Business School Press.

O'Meara, K. (2008). Graduate education and community engagement. *New Directions for Teaching and Learning, 113,* 27–42.

ODI. (2010). *The international registry of organization development professionals and organization development handbook.* Chesterland, OH: Organization Development Institute.

Palmer, P. J. (1998). *The courage to teach: Exploring the inner landscape of a teacher's life.* San Francisco, CA: Jossey-Bass.

Pasmore, W. A., Stymne, B., Shani, A. B., Mohrman, S. A., & Adler, N. (2008). The promise of collaborative management research. In A. B. Shani, S. A. Mohrman, W. A. Pasmore, B. Stymne, & N. Adler (Eds.), *Handbook of collaborative management research.* Los Angeles, CA: SAGE.

Prewitt, K. (2009). Who should do what? Implications for institutional and national leaders. In C. M. Golde & G. Walker (Eds.), *Envisioning the future of doctoral education* (pp. 23–33). San Francisco, CA: Jossey-Bass.

Schein, E. H. (2009). *Helping: How to offer, give and receive help.* San Francisco, CA: Berrett-Koehler.

Schön, D. (1983). *The reflective practitioner: How professionals think in action.* New York, NY: Basic Books.

Schön, D. (1987). *Educating the reflective practitioner.* San Francisco, CA: Jossey-Bass.

Seo, M. -G., Putnam, L. L., & Bartunek, J., M. (2004). Dualities and tensions of planned organizational change. In M. S. Poole & A. H. Van De Ven (Eds.), *Handbook of Organizational Change and Innovation* (pp. 73–107). Oxford, England: Oxford University Press.

Stanley, P. D., & Clinton, J. R. (1992). *Connecting: The mentoring relationships you need to succeed in life.* Colorado Springs, CO: NavPress.

Sweitzer, V. L. (2008). Networking to develop a professional identity: A look at the first-semester experience of doctoral students in business. *New Directions for Teaching & Learning, 2008*(113), 43–56.

Taylor, C. (2009). Heeding the voices of graduate students and postdocs. In C. M. Golde & G. Walker (Eds.), *Envisioning the future of doctoral education* (pp. 46–64). San Francisco, CA: Jossey-Bass.

Taylor, E. W. (2008). Transformative learning theory. *New Directions for Adult & Continuing Education, 119,* 5–15.

Tenkasi, R. V., & Hay, G. W. (2008). Following the second legacy of Aristotle: The scholar-practitioner as an epistemic technician. In A. B. Shani, S. A. Mohrman, W. A. Pasmore, B. Stymne, & N. Alder (Eds.), *Handbook of collaborative management research.* Los Angeles, CA: SAGE.

Thomson, P., & Walker, M. (2010). Doctoral education in context: The changing nature of the doctorate and doctoral students. In M. Walker & P. Thomson (Eds.), *The Routledge doctoral supervisor's companion* (pp. 9–26). New York, NY: Routledge.

Usher, R. (2002). A diversity of doctorates: Fitness for the knowledge economy? *Higher Education Research & Development, 21*(2), 143–153.

Van de Ven, A. H., & Johnson, P. E. (2006). Knowledge for theory and practice. *Academy of Management Review, 31*(4), 802–821.

Varnava-Marouchou, D. (2009). How can students' conceptions of learning improve their learning outcomes? In C. Nygaard, C. Holtham, & N. Courtney (Eds.), *Improving students' learning outcomes* (pp. 97–112). Portland, OR: Copenhagen Business School Press.

Vella, J. (1994). *Learning to listen: Learning to teach*. San Francisco, CA: Jossey-Bass.

Vella, J. (1995). *Training through dialogue: Promoting effective learning and change with adults*. San Francisco, CA: Jossey-Bass.

Vella, J. (2004). *Dialogue education at work*. San Francisco, CA: Jossey-Bass.

Walker, M., & Thomson, P. (Eds.). (2010). *The Routledge doctoral supervisor's companion*. New York, NY: Routledge.

Wasserman, I. C., & Kram, K. E. (2009). Enacting the scholar-practitioner role: An exploration of narratives. *Journal of Applied Behavioral Science, 45*(1), 12–38.

Weinski, M. (2006). *An inquiry into the transformative learning of evangelical theological students in Germany*. Deerfield, IL: Trinity International University.

Williamson, L. (2009). *Outcomes assessment of science & engineering doctor of philosophy (Ph.D.) programs: An exploratory study of prospective influencers in distinguished graduate placement*. Unpublished PhD, TUI University, Cypress, CA.

Worley, C. G., & Feyerherm, A. E. (2003). Reflections on the future of organization. *Journal of Applied Behavioral Science, 39*(1), 97.

ABOUT THE AUTHOR

Deborah Colwill serves in a hybrid position of assistant professor of leadership and director of Institutional Research and Evaluation at Asbury Theological Seminary in Wilmore, KY. Dr. Colwill teaches in the areas of leadership, organization development, and philosophy of education. Her educational background includes a BA in psychology from the University of Minnesota, an MDiv and PhD in education from Trinity International University, and a PhD in organization development from Benedictine University. In addition to her teaching and administration positions, Deborah has served in a variety of leadership and consulting roles within both profit and nonprofit organizations. She has presented at national and international conferences on the topics of leadership, organization development, and education.